The Practice of Local Union Leadership

The Practice of Local Union Leadership

A Study of Five Local Unions

Robert W. Miller
Frederick A. Zeller
Glenn W. Miller

Ohio State University Press

Preface

THIS BOOK examines trade-union leadership at the local union level. It is based on information collected through a systematic study of leadership as practiced in five local union organizations. Its purpose is to broaden understanding of both local union leadership and local union organization. The study is the product of a professional psychologist and two labor economists using an interdisciplinary approach.

The leadership study was conceived originally during the winter of 1960/61 as the result of a practical problem faced by the staff of the Labor Education and Research Service of the Ohio State University. The Labor Service at that time was engaged in developing a program of education for local union members and officers. In working out the program, it was decided that a course in local union leadership would make an important contribution to program goals. Certain questions emerged in attempting to design a leadership course, however. How should local leadership be defined? What are the influences which make local union leadership either easy or difficult? Are local union officers generally successful in leadership? If not, how could leadership be improved? In other words, the problem was what to teach.

In seeking answers to these questions, a need for more information about local union leadership became apparent. Previous studies of union leadership proved either inadequate or out of date, and the opinions of union officials themselves were of little help because of marked lack of agreement. Consequently, it was decided that the needed information could be obtained best through an original investigation of leadership in local unions.

The importance of information about local union leadership extends, of course, far beyond the limits of the practical problem just described. In deciding to proceed with the research, the authors were influenced also by the belief that such a study would contribute to increased understanding of local unions and the practice of leadership, an important social-psychological phenomenon in its own right.

Collection of the data which constitutes the core of the research was begun in the summer of 1961 and completed approximately twelve months later. Five locals from three different international unions served as subjects for the study. The internationals were the United Steelworkers, the United Automobile Workers, and the United Rubber Workers.

Industrial-type internationals were chosen because most of the work of the Labor Service was being done with this type of union at that time, and because it was felt that by concentrating attention on locals of a similar type, there was greater likelihood of achieving a representative picture. The alternative course of studying craft- as well as industrial-type local unions was rejected, because adequate samples of locals of both types could not have been obtained within the limitations of budget and time. Therefore, it seemed wise to conduct a study which would produce more definite findings concerning industrial unions than one which would lead to less adequately substantiated findings concerning both industrial and craft types. Thus, the findings and discussion to follow apply only to industrial-type unions. Moreover, generalizations beyond the sample of five locals included in the study have obvious dangers.

All the locals studied were situated in Columbus, Ohio. Data were collected chiefly by means of interviews and questionnaires which were administered to the major officers of each local and to structured samples of rank-and-file members from each local. Interview and questionnaire responses were obtained from a total of 41 officers and 293 rank-and-file members.

Chapter II contains a description of the characteristics of both the locals and the internationals. A more complete discussion of the method of the study, the samples, and copies of interviews and questionnaires which were used can be found in the appendices.

Originally, our intention did not include the publication of as complete a discussion of the research as the one which follows. The amount of information acquired, along with our judgment that this information—and especially its implications—were important enough to share, led to the decision to report the findings in their present form.

It is our hope that this report will provide useful data and ideas for labor-education practitioners, labor economists, social psychologists, and others interested in the fields of trade-unionism, leadership, and organizational behavior. It is also our hope that this report will be valuable to interested union members and leaders and will provide for them a basis for evaluation of their own organizational attitudes and behavior. All too frequently the results of research are not made available directly to those upon whom such knowledge could have the most meaningful impact for changing the trends and directions of important social behavior.

This study was made possible by a grant-in-aid received from the Ohio State University Development Fund. We express our appreciation to the fund's contributors and to those charged with the fund's administration who responded to our request for financial assistance for the project. Professor S. C.

Kelley, Jr., director of the Ohio State University's Labor Education and Research Service at the time the study was begun, stimulated our interest in the study and offered advice on its general focus and design. Albert Schnaufer and Bernard Jump, students at the Ohio State University at the time the data were collected, conducted most of the interviews and also contributed useful advice and insights concerning the interpretation of the data. Mr. Harry Blaine, a program co-ordinator for the Labor Education and Research Service, read and commented on the entire manuscript. Mr. William Abbott, Education Director, United Rubber Workers, and Professor Norman Keig, University of Florida, also read the manuscript and contributed suggestions which were of considerable assistance. Last, but not least, we are especially appreciative of the co-operation received from those union officers and members who comprise the subjects of our study. Despite the help generously given us by many people, any errors in fact or interpretation are attributable only to the authors.

R.W.M.
F.A.Z.
G.W.M.

Contents

1   The Background and Design of the Research   3

    Local Unions in a Period of Stress   3

    The Need for the Study   5

    The Conceptual Framework of the Study   14

    The Objectives of the Study   21

2   Some Environmental Factors Affecting Leadership Policies and Problems of Local Unions   23

    The Community   23

    The International Unions   25

    The Local Unions   30

    The Employers   34

    The Environment Factors   37

3   Union Members: Their Attitudes and Behavior   39

    Union Democracy   39

    The Need for Followers   41

    The Objective of This Chapter   42

    Member Conceptions of Unionism   43

    Satisfaction Members Get from Unionism   60

    Communications in Local Unions   64

    Differences among the Locals   69

    Summary and Conclusions   73

4 Local Union Officers as Leaders: A Description and Evaluation   75

Characteristics of the Officers   75
Behavior of Officers in Office   76
Officers' Concepts of Union Office   86
Officers' Perceptions of Local Union Goals   89
Identification of Barriers to Goal Achievement   97
Attempts to Remove Barriers to Goal Achievement   106
Evaluation and Conclusions   113

5 The Causes of Unsuccessful Leadership: Factors Which Influence the Performance of Local Union Officers   121

Pressures from the Membership:
The Democratic Context   121
Pressures from the Membership:
Concepts of Unionism   123
Pressures from the Membership:
Desired Form of Member-Officer Relationship   129
Members' Conception of Their Own Union Roles   131
Lack of Member Solidarity   132
Summary: Member Attitudes   134
Personal Limitations of the Officers:
Conceptions of Unionism and Union Leadership   134
Personal Limitations of the Officers:
Lack of Specialized Training and Skills   140
Personal Limitations of the Officers:
Personality and Interpersonal Relations   143
Employer Practices   144
International-Local Union Relationships   148
Trends in Labor Relations   150
A Case Study of Contrasting Leadership Patterns in
Two Local Unions   152
Conclusions   162

6 **Problems and Alternatives Ahead: Implications of the Study** 165

A Brief Summary of Findings 165

Implications of the Findings for the Future Role of Unionism 167

Some Prerequisites for the Survival and Growth of Unionism 179

Leadership and Member Participation in Local Union Organizations 182

Implications of the Findings for Labor Education 195

7 **A Final Comment** 205

Appendixes 209

A The Method of the Study 211
B Union Member Questionnaire 215
C Interview Questions: Union Members 237
D Information Questions: Union Members 241
E Information Questions: Union Officers 251
F Interview Questions: Union Officers 263

Bibliography 269

Index 277

Tables

1   The Formal Education of the Members   47

2   The Problems Identified by the Members   49

3   Means for Accomplishing the Union's Goals That Were Iden-
    tified by the Members   53

4   Local Union Members' Expectations for the International Union   57

5   Respondents' Expectations for Their Local Officers   59

6   Satisfactions Members Get from Their Unions   62

7   Chief Sources of News about Union Affairs   66

8   Chief Sources of Information about Officers' Views   67

9   Members' Chief Sources of Information about the International
    Union's Views   68

10 Amounts of Time Officers Spend on Union Duties   78

11 Activities Which Officers Report Require Most Time   80

12 Performed Activity Which Officers Consider Most Important   84

13 Officers' Explanations of the Difference between Busy and
    Slack Weeks on Union Activities   85

14   Responsibilities of Union Office Officers Consider Most Import-
      ant   87

15   Goals Officers Perceive for Their Local Unions   90

16   Problems Which Officers Perceive as the Greatest Obstacles
      to Achievement of Local Union Goals   98

17   Improvements Officers Feel Their Locals Need to Accomplish
      to Become More Effective   99

18   Ways in Which Officers Attempted to Solve Problems Facing
      Their Locals   107

19   Factors Officers Feel Are Important to Consider When Making
      a Decision   123

20   Officers' Perception of What Members Expect of Them   131

21   Methods by Which Newly Elected Officers Learn to Recognize
      Their Important Responsibilities   140

The Practice of Local Union Leadership

1. The Background and Design of the Research

Local Unions in a Period of Stress

IN AN ERA in which large international unions and even larger business corporations significantly influence the industrial-relations scene, it is increasingly common to hear that local union organizations are declining in influence and importance. Although it is difficult to assess the accuracy of this view, it seems reasonable that, to an unknown degree, such a trend is in progress. It is not certain that the trend is a healthy one for unions or the individual union member, or that it is desirable from a broader socio-political standpoint. Nor is it clear that the trend is inevitable. The authors of the present work have been guided by a belief that local unions are important organizations that need to be strengthened, rather than allowed to decline. For this reason, it is important to recognize and understand problems which may affect them.

As was stated in the Preface, more needs to be known about local unions and local union leadership, because local unions may exert influence as economic institutions and because local unions are vital social organizations of great democratic potential, with highly personal meaning for those who comprise the membership. The local union continues to be the only important organization at the grass-roots of American industrial life possessing a fundamental, if at times latent, ability to satisfy a variety of economic, social, and psychological desires of American workers.

Although local unions have not always been successful in effectuating their potential, the authors believe that they provide a promising means for eventual achievement of workable and meaningful industrial democracy. The aim of the present work is to extend knowledge about practices of local union leadership and acquire insight into present problems and future prospects of the local union as a social, political, and economic institution.

The need for a new assessment of the dynamics of local unionism is vital, especially at a time when rapid social, economic, and technological changes are altering drastically the relationship of workers to their jobs, their unions, and society. The nature of an organization depends on the nature of its membership, the problems which it faces, and the quality of leadership which it enjoys—all of which are subject to change. What was characteristic of local union members ten or fifteen years ago is not as characteristic today. In the face of a changing membership, technology, and social climate, the structures of union organization also have been subject to considerable pressure toward change. Whether local union organizations will succeed eventually in realizing their potentials may depend significantly upon their ability to accommodate change.

Leaders usually play a crucial role in the success of organizations. In order to comprehend fully the workings of organizations, it is important to understand the process of leadership, especially during a period of change, when the strength and effectiveness of organizations depends largely upon flexibility associated with skillful leadership.

The challenge of leadership is to a great extent a challenge of dealing with the problems faced by the organizations and the problems or idiosyncrasies of their members; successfully meeting the challenge is difficult and vital when the nature of the problem areas and the relationship between member and organization is in a state of flux. Under such conditions, the problems which confront the leader are likely to be the ones which must be solved if an organization is to survive or continue in meaningful form. We consider it useful and appropriate to study local union leadership, not only as a means of obtaining information about the process of union leadership, but also as a means of gaining basic insights into local union organizations in a changing society.

The Need for the Study

AN ANALYSIS of previous research pertaining to unions and union leadership helps reveal the need for new approaches to understanding the dynamics of union organizations. A review of this research will sensitize the reader to the need and promote a clearer conceptualization of the specific purposes and objectives of the present study.

Examination of the scholarly literature pertaining to trade-unionism reveals that, though the past fifteen years especially have witnessed publication of numerous books, articles, and monographs dealing with unions and their leaders, the present state of knowledge concerning union leadership is lacking in certain important aspects. The lack is understandable when one considers the focus of previous research and the numerous changes in the last two decades which have helped make the findings of previous research inapplicable to certain current problems.

In the past, scholarly work in the field of trade-unionism has been dominated largely by the institutional approach of the labor economist. Much of the existing body of knowledge concerning unionism therefore centers about union organizations as economic institutions, including such aspects as their structure, their functions, and their policies, and the economic and social implications of these policies. Collective bargaining, contract administration, and the relationship of unions to management, the public, and the government also have received considerable attention.

On the other hand, few works of the institutional type have dealt specifically or in depth with analysis of union leadership or the relationship of union members to their organizations. Works of the institutional type which have dealt with these questions have tended to treat them usually only as aspects of more general "theories" of unionism.[1]

Despite the dominating influence of the institutional approach, there have been some noteworthy attempts to deal more directly with the relationship between the rank-and-file member and his union and with the process of union leadership. The most important of these efforts have focused their attention on the local union organization, have tended to be objectively oriented research studies, and have been the products of the work of social scientists from various fields, including sociology, psychology, and political science, as well as economics. Works of this type have stressed assessment of the motives, attitudes, and opinions of union members, particularly as these personal psychological characteristics tend to reveal the nature of the affiliative bond between member and union. Findings of these studies have furthered understanding of forces influencing the internal cohesion of local

---

[1]Works representative of the institutional approach include classics such as John R. Commons, *The Economics of Collective Action* (New York: Macmillan Co., 1951); Selig Perlman, *A Theory of the Labor Movement* (New York: Macmillan Co., 1929); and R. F. Hoxie, *Trade Unionism in the United States* (New York: D. Appleton and Co., 1917). More recent treatments include Jack Barbash (ed.), *Unions and Union Leadership* (New York: Harper and Bros., 1959); E. Wight Bakke, Clark Kerr, and Charles W. Anrod (eds.), *Unions, Management and the Public* (New York: Harcourt, Brace and Co., 1960; J. B. S. Hardman and Maurice F. Neufeld, *The House of Labor* (New York: Prentice-Hall, 1951); William M. Leiserson, *American Trade Union Democracy* (New York: Columbia University Press, 1951); Richard A. Lester, *As Unions Mature* (Princeton, N. J.: Princeton University Press, 1958); and many others.

unions and have provided information concerning questions of local union democracy and strength and the nature of industrial relations at the local union–employer level.[2]

Among studies which have been directed specifically toward greater insight into leadership, four major categories of approach seem evident: (1) case studies and biographical accounts of the lives and careers of outstanding leaders of American labor;[3] (2) broad discussions of the general personal characteristics, roles, functions, and problems of union leaders at either the national or the local level (usually written from firsthand experience by persons who have had lengthy and intimate acquaintance with the structure and function of trade-unions, and often focusing on leadership in the context of union-management relations or crisis situations such as strikes and organizing drives);[4] (3) works based on research into the personal traits and background characteristics of

---

[2]For example, see Arnold M. Rose, *Union Solidarity* (Minneapolis: University of Minnesota Press, 1952); Hjalmar Rosen and R. A. Rosen, *The Union Member Speaks* (New York: Prentice-Hall, 1955); Joel Seidman, Jack London, Bernard Karsh, and Daisy L. Tagliacozzo, *The Worker Views His Union* (Chicago: University of Chicago Press, 1958); Leonard R. Sayles and George Strauss, *The Local Union: Its Place in the Industrial Plant* (New York: Harper and Bros., 1953); T. V. Purcell, *The Worker Speaks His Mind on Company and Union* (Cambridge, Mass.: Harvard University Press, 1953); T. V. Purcell, *Blue Collar Man* (Cambridge, Mass.; Harvard University Press, 1960); Glenn W. Miller and Ned Rosen, "Members' Attitudes Toward the Shop Steward," *Industrial and Labor Relations Review*, 10 (1957), 516-31; Lois R. Dean, "Union Activity and Dual Loyalty," *Industrial and Labor Relations Review*, 7 (1953-54), 526-36.

[3] For example, see Saul Alinsky, *John L. Lewis: An Unauthorized Biography* (New York: G. P. Putnam Sons, 1949); Irving Howe and B. J. Widick, *The UAW and Walter Reuther* (New York: Random House, 1949); Matthew Josephson, *Sidney Hillman: Statesman of American Labor* (New York: Doubleday and Co., 1952).

[4]See Eli Ginzberg, *The Labor Leader: An Exploratory Study* (New York: Macmillan Co., 1948); also see discussions of leadership in sources such as Jack Barbash, *The Practice of Unionism* (New York: Harper and Bros., 1956), and Clinton S. Golden and Harold J. Ruttenberg, *The Dynamics of Industrial Democracy* (New York: Harper and Bros., 1942).

labor leaders at either the national or the local level;[5] and
(4) discussions and empirical case studies of national and
local union administrative structures and internal operations.[6]
Although these studies have enriched our knowledge of the
men who hold positions of responsibility in unions and have
also provided insight into some of the problems and functions
of union office, they have failed to provide the most appropriate background for a critical analysis and evaluation of
union leadership as an ongoing process subject to the influence
of changing social and economic conditions.

Still another group of publications relating to unions, their
problems, and their leadership appeared in the early sixties.
These studies sprang largely from disillusioned or deeply
doubtful supporters of the union movement of another era.[7]
Each of these raises serious doubts about the ability or willingness of union leadership to cope with the problems of
unions today. Each also looks with some nostalgia upon unions
of an earlier era.

One reason for the shortcomings of certain previous studies
and those cited immediately above is, perhaps, that their
findings tend not to be the product of specific and objective

---

[5]This approach includes works such as C. Wright Mills, *The New
Men of Power* (New York: Harcourt, Brace and Co., 1948); Glenn W.
Miller and Edward J. Stockton, "Local Union Officer—His Background,
Activities and Attitudes," *Labor Law Journal*, 8 (1957), 28-39, Joel
Seidman, Jack London, and Bernard Karsh, "Leadership in a Local
Union," *American Journal of Sociology*, LVI (1950-51), 528-33; Sayles
and Strauss, *op. cit.*

[6]See Arnold S. Tannenbaum and Robert L. Kahn, *Participation in
Union Locals* (Evanston, Ill.: Row, Peterson and Co., 1958); Sayles
and Strauss, *op. cit.*; Seidman *et al.*, *The Worker Views His Union*; Philip
Taft, *The Structure and Government of Trade Unions* (Cambridge,
Mass.: Harvard University Press, 1954). For a discussion of the strengths
and weaknesses of different types of studies of union leadership, see Lois
MacDonald, *Leadership Dynamics and the Trade-Union Leader* (New
York: New York University Press, 1959).

[7]See, for example, Paul Jacobs, *The State of the Union* (New York:
Atheneum Publishers, 1963); and Solomon Barkin, *The Decline of the
Labor Movement* (New York: Fund for the Republic, 1962).

observation of the actual process of leadership in unions, but rather, tend to be findings based on more general impressions of authors with close formal or informal ties to labor. Even though many of these impressions are extremely valuable, they seem to suffer from an orientation shaped by a traditionally conceived context of union problems and administrative structure. A fresh, analytical approach to a problem is difficult to achieve when the problem is embedded in a framework of custom and long-standing expectation. Too often in the case of union leadership, description and evaluation have not been separated carefully enough from judgments (based on knowledge of traditional practices) which are associated with the posited intrinsic value of union organizations. Although leadership needs to be studied within its proper organizational context, there is a serious danger in equating successful leadership practices with the observance of customary organizational procedures.

Another related shortcoming of previous studies of union leadership has been the lack of any systematic definition or conceptual framework against which leadership can be evaluated. Because of this lack, the exact subject under study has not always been clear: the term "leadership" has meant different things to different writers. A quite common approach has been to equate leadership with officeholding at either the national or local level. Objection to this concept will be raised in subsequent pages.

The difficulty with research on union leadership thus seems to stem from two major sources: our understanding is based too largely on intuitive, highly general, and often conflicting conceptions of leadership; and the concepts used are too dependent upon customary ways of perceiving union administrative processes.

A more systematic understanding of leadership as a day-to-day process is needed, particularly as it is practiced in the local union context, where there is more intimate interaction between leaders and followers. It is reasonable to expect that a basic understanding of union organizations and leadership can be furthered through empirical study at the grass-roots, where the member stands in direct contact with his organization. Specifically, it is desirable to have more firm, objective information about what local union officers do in their positions as leaders of the rank and file of American labor. What tasks demand most of their time? How successful are local union officers as leaders? And what are the implications of local union leadership practice for the strength and vigor of union organizations?

In summary, more studies which emphasize newer, systematic conceptions of leadership and its practice in local unions would be desirable. Whereas much past research has stressed personalities, rather than concrete problems and tasks of leadership, it seems important to have research which tends to rely on observation and stresses behaviors and functions, rather than personalities.

When knowledge of the general orientation of previous research into union leadership is combined with awareness of the ever changing relationship between union members and their organizations, the need for additional research becomes even more apparent. As the relationship of member to union changes, and as the surrounding technology and economy change, problems of union leadership change. Leadership demands followers; the behavior of followers, and hence also the success of leadership, will be influenced by the relationship between those followers and the organization. Studies done under previous conditions are not likely to be appropriate for understanding leadership under present conditions. Comparing the unionism of the thirties to that of the fifties, Sidney Lens has commented:

More than anything else it was the mood of the rank and file, so volatile, so susceptible to radical leadership, that made possible the

CIO and the unionization of this period. The "saturation process" had brought them to the point of action. It wasn't the leadership of labor which electrified the rank and file; the workers of this period superimposed a new leadership on top of the old one. . . .

After a few years of heightened interest in union affairs, the mood of the average unionist began slowly to alter. By the late 1950's it had made a full turn around. The subtle social process of the past two decades, which changed the character of the leadership of American labor, also changed the character of the rank and file.[8]

As social, economic, and technological conditions continue to change, the relationship of members to unions will also be likely to vary; thus, in the future union leaders will face even newer tasks.

Although the present authors think that more research into the nature of local unions and local union leadership is important and desirable, we do not underestimate the importance of information which previous studies have revealed. A number of previous studies of the structure, function, and administration of local unions have touched directly or indirectly on the local union leadership process. These studies provide a basis upon which the present research has been built. It seems worthwhile to discuss, in brief, certain of these previous works.

In a now classic study, Sayles and Strauss described the internal operations and characteristics of twenty local unions.[9] Among other topics, the functions of local union officers were discussed in considerable depth. Of importance for the present work was evidence of the time-consuming nature of the responsibilities of union office, the pressures exerted upon officers by the demands of the rank-and-file members, and the realities of the internal politics of the local union organization. The grievance process was noted to be an especially

---

[8]Sidney Lens, *The Crisis of American Labor* (New York: Sagamore Press, 1959), p. 229.

[9]Sayles and Strauss, *op. cit.*

important influence in structuring the roles of the local union officers.

A more recent study of local union member participation by Tannenbaum and Kahn also dealt directly with the process of local union leadership.[10] Among other aspects of local union administration, the study explored the kind and degree of control exercised in the leadership of four local unions, relating the nature of control to factors such as the loyalty and participation of members, the ideology of the local, and the power of the local. In general, the findings of this work indicate that a measure of control, broadly defined as influence in decision-making, seems necessary for the successful practice of leadership in local unions. The stronger, more successful locals were characterized by a greater amount of control, meaning essentially that these locals were able to influence events in such a way as to increase their effectiveness as organizations. Furthermore, sharing of control by both members and officers apparently did not impair such effectiveness but, rather, contributed to it.

Seidman, London, Karsh, and Tagliacozzo studied six local unions.[11] Among problems examined in the study was the role of the local union officer, especially in relation to local union democracy and political structure. The authors made particular note of the existence of channels of pressure and influence which could be utilized by rank-and-file members to influence the course of union affairs. Especially in small industrial-type locals, rank-and-file political pressure on leaders and decision-making was considerable. Another relevant finding of this research was evidence that structural factors such as the size of the local and the security of jobs in the industry were important influences which created leadership problems and placed limits on the power of the local union officer.

---

[10]Tannenbaum and Kahn, *op. cit.*
[11]Seidman *et. al., The Worker Views His Union.*

Studies less directly related to the present research have analyzed and described different orientations of union officers to their responsibilities. For example, Gouldner, on the basis of firsthand observation, separated local union officers into two major types, "business" unionists, and "progressive" unionists.[12] The "business" unionist was characterized as an entrepreneur seeking money, security, and prestige. The "progressive" leader was perceived as more ideologically committed and as placing greater importance on responsibility to the obligations of his office.

A somewhat different categorization has been made by Sayles and Strauss, who divided local union officers into "administrators" and "social leaders."[13] The "administrators" were described as problem-oriented in approach to their positions, efficient, and liking to deal in abstractions, but lacking warmth in relationship with rank-and-file members. The "social leaders," on the other hand, were seen to be primarily interested in personalities and social relationships rather than problems and issues, were relatively inefficient in routine matters of union functioning, but were well liked by rank-and-file members. According to Sayles and Strauss, the two types of leaders did not necessarily differ in their dedication to unionism or their over-all effectiveness as leaders but, rather, simply differed in personal characteristics which influenced their orientation to their positions.

In a somewhat similar vein, Chinoy has dealt with the orientations local union officers take toward their responsibilities, as revealed by the reasons which led them to become union officials.[14] Examination of these reasons led Chinoy to propose the existence of three different types of local union

---

[12]Alvin W. Gouldner, "Attitudes of 'Progressive' Trade Union Leaders," *American Journal of Sociology*, LII (1947), 389-92.

[13]Sayles and Strauss, *op. cit.*

[14]Eli Chinoy, "Local Union Leadership," in Alvin W. Gouldner (ed.), *Studies in Leadership* (New York: Harper and Bros., 1950).

officers: the "accidental," who is pushed into office or acquires it by default (because no one else will take it) but who may in time become dedicated to it; the "ambitious," who seeks union office as a vehicle for personal achievement or aggrandizement; and the "ideological," who is deeply committed to the principles and philosophy of unionism and sees the union office as a "calling."

These studies of local unions, their leaders, and administrative structures represent the core of available knowledge concerning the problems and practices of local union leadership. With the exception of only a few of these findings, the bulk of information concerning union leadership emphasizes personal characteristics of the individuals who fill designated leadership positions, rather than actual leadership functions or behaviors or the conditions which influence these functions and behaviors. The intent of the present work is to attempt to fill some of this gap in understanding the local union as a functioning organization.

The Conceptual Framework of the Study

WE SUGGESTED PREVIOUSLY that studies of union leadership often have not been guided by consistent or adequate conceptions of leadership. One way in which the present study aims to further understanding of the union leadership process is through the use of a systematic conceptual framework which defines leadership and facilitates its analysis and evaluation.

Although there are many conflicting definitions of leadership, we have chosen to follow the approach of Cecil Gibb, who suggests that leadership may be most simply and adequately defined as a relationship within a group characterized by influence or control of one group member over others; in this sense, the term refers to a process or a form of behavior.[15] Gibb illustrates the problem of attempting to study leadership from a context of personality, rather than from one of function or behavior, by pointing out that it may not always be easy to identify the "leader" of a group or organization. Although a common approach is to study officeholders as leaders, within certain groups officeholders may not exert control or influence. Even if chosen as a leader by group members, an individual may or may not perform a leadership function. Studying the personal traits of officeholders thus may provide information about the characteristics of individuals who win elections, but may provide no information about leaders, and further, may add nothing to understanding any actual acts of leadership which may or may not be taking place in a group or organization.

An alternative approach is to define the leader, not as necessarily an officeholder, but as any person around whom group members focus their behavior, the assumption being that such a person would be a source of influence. Such a person might be a disruptive or destructive influence, however, and if so, could not be legitimately termed a leader within the context of the total group, either.

Hence, a major problem for research in leadership is whom to study. Although this will always be true if one is unwilling to equate leadership with officeholding, a behavioral definition of leadership seems to make the problem less acute by providing a criterion which can be used to ascertain whether meaningful leadership does or does not exist. The trend in contemporary leadership research is to study behavior, rather than personalities.

One way of using the behavioral approach is to determine whether any acts of positive influence are taking place in a group. If they are, they may be analyzed and described and

[15]Cecil A. Gibb, "Leadership," in Gardner Lindzey (ed.), *Handbook of Social Psychology*, Vol. II (Reading, Mass.: Addison, Wesley Publishing Co., 1954).

their source ascertained; or they may be evaluated against an agreed-upon definition of what constitutes successful leader behavior. No risky assumptions that certain persons are necessarily leaders need be made; the whole topic is removed from the context of a subjective orientation, which makes leadership an indefinable quality of an individual or a set of personal psychological traits, and is placed in a more objective framework which permits rational assessments to be made and useful conclusions concerning ways of improving leadership to be drawn. The present study attempts to employ a behavioral approach in assessing the nature of leadership in local unions.

Choosing to study leader behavior, rather than nominal leaders, does not solve fully the practical problem of whose behavior to study. Behavior is a product of the functioning of individuals and cannot be studied in isolation from individuals. A logical implication of the behavioral approach to leadership is that all behavior in a group or organization is worthy of study and evaluation. Technically, every member of a group is a potential source of influence and leader behavior: to adhere strictly to a behavioral approach, the behavior of every member would have to be studied and evaluated. To be realistic, however, in a complex organization of any size, only a certain few members are likely to be in a position to exert meaningful influence. In addition, for practical reasons research in large organizations must be confined to the study of a manageable number of members.

The present study deals with this problem by evaluating the behavior of the top elected officials of selected local unions against a formal behavioral criterion of leadership. Our reasoning is that in a local union, as a complex potentially democratic organization, the probability is that members look to elected officials for leadership. It is therefore both likely and proper for elected officials to be the prime source of leader behavior; it is also important to know whether or not they *are* a source of leader behavior. This research attempts to describe the behavior of the local union officers, evaluate it against a formal definition of leadership, analyze the causative factors giving rise to the behavior, and spell out the implications of the behavior for the strength and effectiveness of the locals. Thus, the study explores whether local union officers are successful as leaders of their organizations and, if not, why not. Personal characteristics of officers receive only limited attention and only for the purpose of helping us to explain success or failure in the leadership endeavor.

A major problem in designing the study was the need for an adequate behavioral definition of leadership. Considering the relative lack of information about leadership as a process in local unions, it was decided that a broad definition would be less likely to result in a technically narrow interpretation and evaluation of the behavior of the local union officers. The definition decided upon was modeled after the work of John Hemphill.[16] For purposes of this study, local union leadership was defined as behavior which influences a local union toward achievement of its goals.

Definitions of group and organization were also needed, because leadership, as so defined, is an integral and dependent aspect of the nature of the context in which it occurs. In a small, homogeneous, intimate context characterized by face-to-face interaction between leader and followers, there would be maximum opportunity for successful influence to be exerted by a leader. Such a context is normally called a group. In a larger, more impersonal type of context without face-to-face contact between members, normally called an organization, leadership is more difficult. In order to analyze leadership in local unions adequately, it is helpful therefore to know whether locals more nearly approximate groups or organi-

---

[16]John K. Hemphill, *Theory of Leadership* (Columbus, O.: Ohio State University Personnel Research Board, 1952).

zations. The following specific definitions were chosen for purposes of such analysis: a *group* consists of two or more persons with interdependent relationships, the behavior of each member influencing the behavior of each of the other members, and with a shared ideology in the form of a set of beliefs, values, and norms which regulates mutual conduct; an *organization* is an integrated system of interrelated groups formed to accomplish a stated objective.[17]

If the context in which leadership is attempted is a mere collection of individuals which approximates neither the definition of group or organization, leadership would be an extremely difficult, if not altogether impossible, task. Although leadership would be easier in an organizational setting, the problems would still be obviously more complex there than in a simpler group setting. At the time the research was planned, it seemed reasonable to assume that most local unions would fit our definition of organization, some would more nearly approximate groups, and some would more nearly approximate mere collections.

Use of words such as solidarity and brotherhood in referring to unions would seem to reveal a tendency on the part of union officials, in particular, to think of unions as groups and to follow practices most appropriate for groups. Based on our research, however, we suggest that it is uncertain that local unions do, in fact, fit our definition of the group. During the course of the study, the issue of whether locals are groups, organizations, or mere collections became a vital question which had to be considered an integral aspect of a study of union leadership.

Three behavioral components of leadership, as defined above, played a major role in the actual design of the research. These three components or separate leadership "acts"

---

[17]David Krech, Richard S. Crutchfield, and Egerton L. Ballachey, *Individual in Society* (New York: McGraw-Hill Book Co., 1962), pp. 383-84.

must necessarily be involved in any instance of successful leadership.

The first component of leadership is perception or identification of organizational goals. In order to influence a local union toward the achievement of its goals, a potential leader must explicitly or implicitly recognize appropriate goals. Within the democratic context of the local union, goals should be set primarily by the membership. It is hence a task of the potential local union leader to recognize the goals that members seek through their union.

Even in a democratic setting, a successful leader may at times have to influence the goals of the members, rather than depend upon inadequately formulated, poorly stated, or inappropriate desires. In such case, it may be necessary for the leader to participate actively in the actual setting of goals. This can be done by influencing members' opinions concerning goals in ways which would best promote organizational effectiveness. In actual practice, members may not always have the insight, ability, or interest to designate their goals formally; in many instances, the setting of goals is quite properly a product of the interacting influences of leaders and members.

As a potential leader of a democratic organization, a local union officer should, however, accurately reflect the goals of the membership when these are once set, no matter what the extent of his initial influence in arriving at the goals. It is a specific objective of this study to evaluate the extent to which top elected officers accurately reflect the goals which local union members consciously perceive for their organization.

The second necessary component of leadership is the perception or identification of significant problems or barriers which prevent achievement of the goals of the local. Our reasoning here is that if there were no problems (broadly defined) standing in the way of group goal attainment, there would be no need for a leader: there would be no need for behavior aimed at moving an organization toward its goals under circumstances of immediate, free, and unrestricted satisfaction of all goals. Such circumstances would be characteristic if no problems stood in the way of goal achievement. We mean to define a problem or barrier in the broadest sense —to include, not only problems external to a union, (such as management might pose) but also problems within a union (such as a lack of solidarity might create). Another of the specific objectives of this study is to evaluate the extent to which top elected local union officers accurately identify the important problems preventing achievement of local union goals.

The third and last component of leadership is defined as behavior which is influential in stimulating action to remove problems preventing attainment of the goals of the local. This is the important, indispensable last step which completes the sequence of acts making up the behavior we call leadership. This culminating step is to a great degree a product of the relationship between the potential leader and the local union members. It is the active, overt essence of leadership in that the potential leader *must* be able to exert control, or influence over others. He must be able to "lead" them toward the removal of barriers preventing achievement of agreed-upon goals.

The essence of leadership is, not simply the possession of certain personal qualities, nor the existence of a simple relationship between a potential leader and potential followers, but rather, a dynamic, active process of influence through which the leader stimulates followers to behave in such a way as to move a group toward its goals. The process may depend upon having a proper relationship between leader and followers, but potential leadership does not become actual leadership until influencing others, or "leading" them, becomes a fact. A third specific objective of this study is to assess the extent to which top elected local union officers engage in acts of influence aimed at removing barriers to the achievement of local union goals.

The Objectives of the Study

SPECIFIC OBJECTIVES of the present study are the following:

1. to describe the behavior of local union officers in performance of union responsibilities

2. to ascertain the extent to which local union officers successfully accomplish the three behavioral components of leadership

   a) to evaluate the extent to which local union officers accurately reflect the goals which local union members consciously perceive for their organization

   b) to evaluate the extent to which local union officers accurately identify the important problems preventing achievement of local union goals

   c) to evaluate the extent to which local union officers engage in acts of influence aimed at solving problems preventing achievement of local union goals

3. to explore and analyze factors which determine the extent to which local union officers are successful in leadership

4. to discuss implications of problems of local union leadership for the future of trade-unionism

2. Some Environmental Factors Affecting Leadership Policies and Problems of Local Unions

THE POLICIES, PROGRAMS, AND PROBLEMS which have implications for leadership within a local union may be affected, among other factors, by the community in which the local operates, the international of which it is a part, and the managerial organization with which it deals. Further, the sample of local unions selected for study will influence the findings. The size of the locals, level of member education, the industry involved, ages of members, and other conditions in all likelihood will affect the goals, policies, and practices noted. Each of these major influencing factors will be examined in order to note its possible influence on local union leadership problems.

The Community

FOR THE LOCALS on which this study is based, the impact of the geographic location, though most difficult to measure, probably serves to make local union leadership more difficult. The city in which they are located is not, nor has it ever been, a strongly prounion community. The metropolitan area, nearing seven hundred thousand at the time of the 1960 census, traditionally has been a center of education, government, distribution, and office-type undertakings, such as insurance. White-collar work has been and continues to be a major source of employment. As might be expected with such an employment picture, unemployment has not plagued the city as much as it has many other areas in the state or the nation, and this greater degree of economic security may have served to make workers in the area a less militant group than might be found under other conditions.

While local industries such as construction, printing, and transportation have been unionized (with a sprinkling of membership elsewhere up to World War II), unions in these organized areas exercised no strong influence on public attitudes or policies. Essentially, the attitude of the public has been, and continues to be, one characterized by indifference, lack of understanding, or varying degrees of animosity toward the union movement.

To a considerable extent, the viewpoint attributed to the city area is found throughout the state, with the exception of the areas in which mining and manufacturing predominate. To date, despite its industrial development and considerable unionization, the state has not been in any real sense prolabor. Nor has it, on the other hand, been a clearly antilabor state.

For example, the state legislature has never enacted a state labor-relations act similar to the Wagner Act. On the other hand, by a referendum vote a "right to work" measure was turned down overwhelmingly in 1958. The state has no legislation similar to the federal Norris–LaGuardia Act, and injunctions in labor disputes emanate frequently from state courts. No state-created machinery for the settlement of labor disputes is operative. On the other side of the ledger, labor in the state has had the benefit of reasonably acceptable legislation dealing with workmen's compensation and unemployment compensation. While a minimum-wage law has been on the statute books for a quarter-century, it is limited and inadequate in coverage: the level of protection offered, even in the covered industries, is far below federal levels.

Thus, in the area of public policy as shown through state-enacted legislation, the state has not proved to be a consistently outstanding or a consistently poor example. From the union officer's point of view, it leaves much to be desired, but this probably is true of every state. While unions occasionally have had an influence on public attitudes and politics, as a whole the state has not been extreme in either direction, although clearly leaning toward conservatism. The general climate of public opinion as evidenced by labor legislation has been somewhat, but not markedly, dampening, as far as union activity is concerned.

As for the city and the surrounding area, it fits the public-attitude picture outlined for the state. The area has experienced considerable influx of manufacturing industry in recent years, but the traditional white-collar and professional attitudes toward group activity have remained. Further, the 1960 census still showed nearly 50 per cent of employment in white-collar work.

The importance of general public attitudes and of news and opinion-forming media is conjectural as far as the administrative problems of local unions are concerned. Usually examples can be cited to prove almost any degree of influence which is postulated. It is suggested, however, that the conservative attitudes of the press and the general public of the city and the surrounding area probably do create problems for the officers of local unions in the area, in the sense that workers' collective action through the medium of a union is not encouraged and in some instances may even be discouraged.

The International Unions

IN THIS STUDY, local unions of the steelworkers, the automobile workers, and the rubber workers were examined. All three are progressive, well-established products of the CIO upsurge of the thirties; each is an example of international union that endeavors to assist its locals in meeting the problems which they face in negotiations, local union administration, grievance-handling, and the like. The functions of the staff representative, the practice of pattern bargaining, and assistance in late stages of grievance-processing are well-known services of internationals to their locals, designed in part as means of assisting the locals.

The amount and quality of service and supervision from the international unions varies among the five locals, however. Two of the locals (locals A and B),[1] serviced by the same international representative, receive close supervision and, generally, are able to obtain advice, information, or whatever else is needed from the international representative upon request. Their international representative usually attends all of the meetings of the executive board of the local as well as the regular and special membership meetings. In addition, the officers from locals A and B report that he can be contacted by telephone almost anytime and will meet with them in their homes, or other convenient places, to discuss any problems that arise. As a matter of fact, several of the executive-board members of these two locals offered the suggestion that the international representative was around almost too much; they would prefer a higher degree of independence from the international. As might be inferred, this representative had comparatively few locals to deal with (less than ten). Further, this reflects the policy of the international of providing close and continuous supervision and services for its locals.

In contrast to this, locals C and D, also serviced by the same international representative, received relatively little

---

[1] In order to preserve the anonymity of the locals, they are referred to as locals A, B, C, D, and E throughout the text of this report. Further, the locals, (as designated by letters) are not identified with their present internationals for the same reason.

international union supervision and services. It is the consensus of the executive boards of both these locals that much more supervision and service from the international is needed by the locals if they are to resolve a number of long-standing problems. In this case, the international representative only occasionally attends executive-board or membership meetings. For the most part, he does not make an appearance on the local scene in response to requests for information or service until days—sometimes even weeks—elapse, unless the local situation is characterized by crisis.[2] Additionally, he usually cannot be reached by telephone; hence, it frequently is necessary for the local to contact him through a third party. This situation is the outcome of the international representative's far-flung territory. He is compelled to travel continually and spend a minimum amount of time at any one place. This situation reflects the international union's policy of encouraging local union autonomy.

The fifth local, local E, is affiliated with an international that usually attempts to provide close supervision and control. It was found that the international representative attends most, if not all, of the meetings, can be reached easily by telephone, and is available to the local when it requests assistance. However, most of the officers of this local reported a need for more help from the international than they were getting. In this case, the problem is that local officers doubt the competence of the international representative. One officer from this local observed: "The international rep is just like us, and that's the problem, because we need someone better than we are." Several of the officers implied that the international representative seemed too friendly with company

---

[2]The executive board from local D related that only once did the international representative make an appearance within twenty-four hours after his presence was requested. At the time, a bitter wildcat strike was in progress. When he arrived, he reportedly dealt with all of the parties involved in a very competent fashion, and the strike ended shortly thereafter.

officials; they said that several times he had been observed drinking with them. Therefore, even though the policy of the international is to provide a great deal of top-down service, union officers believe that the local is not adequately serviced because of the person representing the international.

Still another difference among the various internationals is that related to collective bargaining. Three locals, locals C, D, and E, bargain according to patterns that are established by the international. While some deviations from the patterns are permitted in order to deal with local peculiarities, the international union plays an important role in the process of collective bargaining itself.

On the other hand, locals A and B are free to bargain much as they see fit. In so doing, they may call upon the international for assistance, or it may be customary for such assistance to be provided, but actual control of the bargaining process (on the union's side) resides with the local. An incident demonstrating the ability of the local to exert ultimate control was related by one of the officers from local B:

> Our committee, with the international representative, met with the company. We knew what the members wanted and we were going to get as much of it as we could. Our man from the international decided something else—he thought we could get some favorable changes in job rules. We didn't care if he tried to get them, but he got into a bad argument with a company man and they called each other names. We saw right away that wasn't going to make our job any easier, so we asked for a recess. The union committee and the representative met and we told him to stay out from here on. He did, and we got the contract settled without hard feelings. He's a good man, but he and the company man have a long history of bad feelings.

In this instance, the local demonstrated its ability to exert control by removing the only international representative from the bargaining process.

Differences in the nature of the relationships between the international and the local such as those described have implications for the practice of leadership. For example, local officers who can turn to the international representative for information, advice, or technical assistance when confronted by organizational and industrial-relations problems usually will be in a better position to satisfy their members and, hence, will be more likely to retain their offices. Local officers who are compelled to deal with most problems, especially technical problems, without benefit of international assistance are likely to fail more frequently and, hence, disappoint their constituents oftener. It is likely they will be in the position of having to spend disproportionate amounts of time dealing with day-to-day problems which have limited significance for the local union as an organization while they are in office and, also, will be turned out of office more frequently. Implications such as these will be spelled out in greater detail in later chapters.

Each of the internationals has a newspaper—judged by the authors, in comparison with other union papers, to be a reasonably good one—which is used to build *esprit de corps* among members, as well as to convey information about the union and public affairs. There is in the *Rubber Worker, Steel Labor,* and *UAW Solidarity* a major effort to build union attachment and loyalty. We will demonstrate later that attitudes of union members surveyed suggest that the efforts have not been highly successful. Even so, the locals studied herein were of internationals whose publications stand well in comparison with other such journals. While the publications may be inadequate by absolute standards, they are quite satisfactory on a comparative basis.

Also, these internationals have sought to assist meeting the administrative problems of locals through education programs. Each has sought to provide, in co-operation with labor-education services of universities or alone, short-course and conference training in a variety of subjects related to the effective administration of the union local. "Courses" in union history, grievance-handling, collective bargaining, union administration, labor legislation, and the like have been offered from time to time. Most of the persons attending these education programs have been officers, committee members, or people in some other position of influence in the local of which they are a member, and by which they usually are sent to the school.

It is true that training of local union officers has grown rapidly in recent years in many unions. However, the three internationals with locals involved in this study have been more active than most unions. Thus, the locals surveyed had available some opportunity of training for their officers; most of the officers in this study had taken advantage of such opportunities.

All three of the internationals also have a top leadership and staff which is able to develop information and materials for the locals. These data and information are disseminated through union newspapers, other publications, and the staff representatives servicing the locals. While it is true, as will be noted later, that the members of the locals showed a marked lack of knowledge of, and interest in, their union, this did not spring from a lack of interest or effort by the parent union.

It might be pointed out that it is likely the education programs, the publications, and the services of staff representatives are the products of the movement-oriented, or at least organization-oriented, members of the local and international hierarchies. The approach and the argument that may be persuasive to such persons may well fall ineffectively on the ears of the average member.

The Local Unions

THE SIZE OF THE LOCALS STUDIED does not set them apart from most unions: none of them was especially large or small, with an average membership of around five hundred and a range or from four hundred to seven hundred. It is obvious that there will be more complex problems of communication and administration in a larger union, although a large local is likely to have one or more full-time officers. None of the locals in this study had full-time officers. All were directed by persons whose primary activity was a job in the shop; thus, the administration of the local was "extracurricular" activity. While the operation of the local may suffer from this fact, the locals are not distinctive for this reason. The typical union local in the nation is administered under similar circumstances.

A factor judged to be of some importance is the skill composition of the membership. The bulk of the members of all locals studied are in mass-production types of activity in which skilled jobs are not common. By their own estimate, nearly three-fourths of the respondent members considered their jobs to be either semi-skilled or unskilled, and it is likely that most persons may see their jobs as more demanding than another person might. Roughly one-fourth of the members surveyed considered their jobs skilled.

The distributions of members among the unskilled, semi-skilled, and skilled categories probably serves to enhance the leadership problems of local officers. A small local centered on a common skill may provide the basis for a more cohesive organization.[3] Here again the skill-mix of the membership in the locals studied does not make the locals unusual; the small single-craft local is not typical of organized labor in the geographic area of the study, or in the nation.

Some of the personal characteristics of the members suggest no particular problems, while others do. Five-sixths of the respondents were men, most of whom were married. Almost

---

[3]It is of course recognized that organizational cohesion depends upon many different factors, some of which are attitudinal, while others are structural. See, for example, Seymour Martin Lipset, Martin A. Trow, and James S. Coleman, *Union Democracy* (Garden City, N. Y.: Anchor Books, 1962).

exactly half were forty years of age or more, and most of them were not newcomers to the union movement. Not one of the respondents had been a union member for less than one year; over half had been members for more than ten years. About 40 per cent had been members of their present local for at least ten years. Thus, in no sense was there a problem of an inexperienced membership that had not had ample opportunity to become familiar with the work of a union.

While not a highly distinguishing factor, the average level of formal education of the respondent member is judged to have contributed to the problems of the local officers. Almost one-third of the members reported formal schooling of not more than eight grades. Three-fifths of the remainder had not completed high school. Put differently, only a few more than a fourth of those who responded had as much as twelve years of formal schooling. The general level of schooling probably was such as to intensify the problem of effective leadership, since those with little formal education are not likely to have highly developed skills useful for communications, interpersonal and organizational relations, and for sorting realistic from unrealistic expectations.

Certain differences in personal characteristics of the members exist among the different locals. Whereas almost all the members of locals A, B, C, and D are white, a majority of the members of E is Negro. Similarly, almost all of the officers of local E are Negroes. In our judgment, many attitudinal differences in that local stem from the racial difference. Thus, the officers are confronted by a divisive factor in terms of the local union organization; they can do comparatively little to cope with the problem in the short run. Many of the white minority interpret the Negro majority as a sign of white-member exploitation by the organization. Quite a few of the white members who were interviewed said the Negro members discriminated against them; some of them also said they believe the company discriminates against the Negroes. Without doubt, the lines drawn on the basis of racial differences in this local accentuate the need for leadership (in order to build a cohesive organization) and make its development more difficult. In addition, the work performed by most of the members of local E is heavy manual labor, compared to considerably less fatiguing jobs performed by most of the members of the other locals. Members of the executive board pointed out the heavy labor as a principal reason for the near impossibility of developing a highly spirited, active membership.

The characteristics of many members in two other locals (locals C and D) are also somewhat unusual. Rather than a division along racial lines, the members are divided noticeably along line of geographic origin into roughly two groups: those who have been long-time residents of the city or the surrounding area, and those who have moved to the city from the southern part of the state or nearby southeastern states within, say, the past fifteen years. The "natives" have industrial traditions and outlooks. Frequently, they hold the higher skilled jobs within the plant, and they are more than proportionately represented on the executive boards of the two locals. They, more than the "immigrants," are willing to concede the fact and morality of the employer's existence and rights, while adhering to their own right to be included in the process of making industrial-relations decisions. On the other hand, the immigrants have either (sometimes both) agricultural or coal-mining traditions and outlooks. The presence of the ex–coal miners is attributable to the decline of that industry and the movement to metropolitan areas of workers seeking employment. Most of the former coal miners are schooled in the militant ways of the United Mine Workers and look askance at the conciliatory measures sometimes favored by the natives. Representative of this attitude was the comment of one during an interview who said, "This isn't a union I belong to now. The mine workers are used to fighting and they don't stop until they get what's fair. But this outfit is always looking for a way to agree with the company."

Many of the members with agricultural backgrounds somewhat surprisingly have been sold on the idea (the identity of the "seller" is unknown) that the function of the union is to fight the employer. Thus, they are allies of the former coal miners. (At the same time, it must be pointed out that many of the immigrants reported they were both farmers and coal miners previous to their arrival in the metropolitan area; therefore, the attitudinal similarity of the former farmers and coal miners may be similar in origin as well as in nature.) For the most part, the coalition group favors vigorous, militant union action against the employer, and usually they are disappointed, since the locals are controlled by the more moderate natives. Again, the differences between the natives and the immigrants are not easily resolvable: they stem from differences in the socialization process itself; they constitute difficulties for the emergence of leadership.

With respect to personal characteristics, then, those possessed by the members from locals C, D, and E are especially problematic with respect to the leadership function. The low educational levels attained by the typical member are problematic for them all.

The Employers

THE NATURE of the employing organization and the attitudes found therein have a major effect on employee and union attitudes; belligerence builds belligerence, and a sympathetic and employee-oriented management will elicit a more flexible approach from the workers.[4]

---

[4]Leonard R. Sayles and George Strauss, *The Local Union: Its Place in the Industrial Plant* (New York: Harper and Bros., 1953) pp. 14-24. See also, Clinton Golden and Harold Ruttenberg, *The Dynamics of Industrial Democracy* (New York: Harper and Bros., 1942).

The employers of the union members manifested different attitudes toward the unions, ranging between almost complete acceptance—even encouragement—and discouragement. The employers of the members of local unions A and C are sympathetic toward the union's existence. For example, they permit union officers to have considerable freedom in moving around the shop in order to communicate with the members and discuss their problems with them. Also, they have demonstrated their acceptance of the union's role in other ways. One of them inevitably consults with the top local officers before any extra-contractual changes affecting workers are announced officially. In fact, this employer usually permits the top officers to make unofficial announcements of such changes before official notice is given. This practice, by one company official's own admission, is intended to demonstrate to the members the employer's willingness to accept the union as a meaningful unit in the industrial-relations decision-making process. As far as we could determine, this practice is genuine in the following sense: the suggestions of the local officers are carefully considered, and not infrequently embodied, in the final decision. The other employer makes the company lunchroom available for union committee meetings and meetings of the officers. Therefore, it is possible for committeemen and officers working several different shifts to meet conveniently to dispose of official business as it arises.

Nevertheless, the good relations generally enjoyed by employers and locals A and C don't preclude occasional, serious disharmony. Within recent years, both locals have conducted fairly long strikes. However, the behavior of both parties at such times has been moderate, thus precluding development of strongly held animosity and hostility carried over to the post-strike periods.

The employers of the members of locals D and E are of a different mind. Both resent the existence of the union and refuse to grant recognition and approval except as required by law. In the usual case, the officers of locals D and E are not permitted to discuss union business in the plant apart from that specified in the contract (e.g., the handling of grievances). These employers are extremely legalistic in their approach to the contract. Whereas the employers of the members of locals A and C are willing to seek mutually satisfactory solutions for problems which arise from day to day, these employers frequently seek refuge in finely drawn, technically precise, interpretations of the contract. Not unexpectedly, this gives rise to the members' attempts to fight fire with fire. Accordingly, both locals seem constantly to be dealing with disproportionately large numbers of grievances. Further, an exceptionally large number of the grievances are taken to arbitration. The situation has been especially acute in local D. Additionally, in that local, the employer frequently has followed the practice of delaying settlement of the grievances as long as possible. Dissatisfaction with the grievance-settlement process has led to several wildcat strikes in recent years in local D. All in all, bad feelings between local D and its employer have been assiduously cultivated in the past and remain in the present to complicate the development of a co-operative relationship.

The relationship between the employer and local B is less extreme than those described above. The relationship has been neither particularly good nor bad.

Although all of the five companies had some workers laid off at the time the data were collected, the economic position of the employers of the members of locals B and E was especially tenuous. Local E's industry had been declining for some time. Unless the firm is able to adapt to some other line of manufacture, the layoffs will continue; it is unlikely that the workers who are laid off will ever be recalled. Local B's employer apparently was unable to compete in an otherwise healthy industry; hence, the company's sales volume and number of employees were both decreasing. Here again, the possibility of recall is slight unless some key changes are made in the company's pattern of operations.

From the foregoing description, it is obvious that the differences among the employers' attitudes and economic positions will have different ramifications for the local unions and their officers. Although the point will be made in greater detail in a later chapter, the employers' positions and industrial-relations policies have significant effect on the character, presence, and need for leadership. Equally obvious is the local officers' incapability to reshape that part of the environment contributed by the employers. While adept and intelligent local officers may be successful in developing greater understanding of the workers' needs and problems by management, they can do comparatively little about structural changes in the economy. The essential point is that the employer is an integral component of the complex out of which local union leadership must emerge if it is to exist at all.

The Environment Factors

TAKEN AS A WHOLE, the environmental factors discussed in this chapter probably are such as to make the problems of local union leadership somewhat more difficult in some of the locals than in others.

Differences in the amount of help provided to the locals by the internationals, the attitudes of employers, and the socio-economic backgrounds of the members undoubtedly were responsible for differences in the leadership environment among the five locals. Because of these differences, the study of local leadership is made more difficult. If, for example, one observes a higher caliber of leadership in one local union than in another, this may be the result either of individuals with different degrees of talent serving in leadership roles, or individuals with equal talents confronted by problems of different magnitudes. A number of other alternative explanations are possible as well.

But problems for local leaders were found in all of the locals. The absence of a skill-nexus, the moderately large size of the locals, and the relatively low level of formal education —all are considered to be deterrent factors. These are not pointed out in any critical sense, for the conditions are to a great extent beyond the control of any one individual or union body. Some types of work or places of employment do not require many skilled workers, and the workers can do nothing about it; some workers are not, or cannot be, well educated. But, whether fault is involved or not, leadership practices in such a union may be affected adversely by such conditions.

3. Union Members: Their Attitudes and Behavior

Union Democracy

OF ALL COMPONENTS of the environment importantly influencing leader behavior, none is more important than the local membership. This is true for two reasons: the democratic structure of union organizations, and the leader's need for followers.

While it is commonplace to observe that most unions fail to achieve a large measure of substantive democracy, it is true that almost all of them have formal provision for democratic procedures. Although it is possible for members to be denied access to these procedures, this is not a typical situation. Statutory safeguards, as well as unionists' high regard for democracy, are factors explaining the typical accessibility of democratic procedures to interested members.

One such democratic procedure, the right of members to vote for their local officers, is of particular importance for the study of leader behavior. If we are to compare the behavior of elected officers to a leadership-behavior model, an understanding of the coincidence (or its absence) of observed behavior and model behavior requires us to pay attention to the reasons behind the observed behavior. Members who are dissatisfied with their officers can sooner or later remove them from office. If officers are motivated primarily to retain their offices, their behavior, in most cases at least, must coincide reasonably well with member expectations. This is not to say that officers unerringly should or do follow every inclination and whim manifested by the members. Rather, officers and members should interact with each other, exchanging information and views, and modifying their positions and attitudes in accord with the directions suggested by the outcome of mutual rational persuasion. Clearly, this is part of the leadership process.

The ability of officers and members to influence each other, however, depends upon how near together or far apart their views are, how tenaciously these views are held, and how relatively efficient officers have been in dealing with problem situations perceived by the members. If the majority of voting members reach negative conclusions about their officers' positions and behavior, they may respond by replacing them. Therefore, the officer who desires to retain his position must constantly be aware of his dependence upon his constituents; moreover, he must modify his behavior to reach approximate correspondence with that expected of him, or he must modify member expectations. Consequently, in one way or another, the attitudes, evaluations, and behavior of the members of a democratic local union impinge on the elected officer and may be expected to affect his own attitudes, evaluations, and behavior. But, by implication, the matter of key significance for this study is the extent of difficulty, or facility, for the leadership process posed by the members and their expectations. For example, if most members demand compliance with unchanging expectations, and if these expectations are at odds with reality, leadership as we have defined it would have been dealt an almost fatal blow. Oppositely, the members could be characterized as having realistic expectations and being amenable to the influence of others. Seemingly, this would facilitate the process of leadership.

The Need for Followers

APART FROM the characteristic trade-union potentiality for direct membership control, there is reason to place heavy emphasis on the determination and analysis of member attitudes and behavior in a study of local union leadership. The reason is the leader's need for followers.

Leadership cannot occur unless there are followers. Since the followers must permit themselves to be led and presumably will give their permission only if they agree with the objectives of the leadership, the leader's behavior is at least influenced by,[1] and made effective or ineffective by, the followers' attitudes and expectations. As indicated above, the followers' attitudes and expectations may be modified as the result of leadership acts, but at any moment the process of leadership is circumscribed by the wishes and desires of the followers. The nature of this circumscription forms the immediate context of leader behavior; it may encourage or repress that behavior.

It has been stated above (in Chapter I) that leadership is a relatively simple or a relatively difficult task, depending upon the degree of organization of the members. It is most difficult if the members are a mere collection of individuals, less difficult if they have the characteristics of organizational members, and least difficult if they are group members. The distinction among these three possibilities has not received the attention it deserves by local union analysts; yet the organizational structure so conceived has powerful implica-

---

[1]The rigidity of the circumscription may, of course, vary with different issues confronting the organization. See, for example, Seymour Martin Lipset, Introduction, in Eden Paul and Cedar Paul (trans.), Robert Michels' *Political Parties* (New York: Collier Books, 1962), pp. 30-32.

tions for leader behavior. Several hypothetical examples will make this clear.

Members could be described as a mere collection of individuals if they are concerned only with the implications of the union for themselves as individuals. In the extreme case, the prevalence of selfish orientation could result in the members' unwillingness to recognize any responsibilities to the organization unless their own interests are involved. If so, it would be difficult, perhaps impossible, for these members to be led, because they have no common reason to join together. If this condition were identified empirically, the union would be neither an organization nor a group, under our definition of these terms.

On the other hand, members of a local union who are interested in their own welfare but who also recognize their responsibility for the welfare of others in exchange for their own right to welfare can be led, since they are joined together by a system of mutual rights and responsibilities: the members are characterized by a state of interdependence. If their relationship is personal and tenacious, they are referred to as members of a group; if it is impersonal and relatively weak, the members are said to be part of an organization.

In the former case (a collection of individuals), leadership will be difficult until such time as groups or organizations are formed. Therefore, officers' efforts to form such structures are themselves a type of leader behavior. But leadership is an easier task once the group or organization exists, because at that time the members perceive a common goal structure and, more importantly, perceive the need for collective, interrelated action. Then they are more capable of being led.

The Objective of This Chapter

THE MEMBERS, therefore, are a vital aspect of the leadership process, both because they have the power to name those most likely to attempt leader acts and because their relationship to the union affects the ease or difficulty of the leaders' tasks.

Accordingly, the objective of this chapter is to describe and analyze the attitudinal and organizational characteristics of the members included in the five samples as they are relevant to the leadership process. We shall examine the nature and strength of the members' attitudes and behavior that appear to be of significance for their officers as leaders and estimate the members' organization, group, or collection characteristics. Initially, we will discuss the findings that describe the members' concepts of unionism, including their attitudes toward union goals, problems, methods of dealing with problems, and organizational roles. Next, we will discuss the satisfactions members say they get from union membership. This will be followed by discussion of communications within the five locals. Finally, we will point out the most important differences among the locals with respect to leadership.

The questions, which were employed in both membership interviews and questionnaires, were designed to gather information about the members' concepts of unionism, the extent of membership participation in local union affairs, the communications structure within local unions, and the kinds of satisfactions which workers derive from union membership. It will be recognized immediately that these questions have been utilized as the cores of a number of pathfinding, valuable studies of union members. The following presentation makes no claim for originality in its basic approach; it is intended to serve as the background for the study of leadership in the five local unions that comprise the subjects for this study.

Member Conceptions of Unionism

IN ORDER TO DETERMINE the broad outlines of membership attitudes and expectations with regard to union affiliations, the members in the samples were asked questions designed to elicit their positions as to the range of union goals, the problems that seem to inhibit the accomplishment of those goals, the available organizational resources to be used to deal with these problems, and the respective roles of the local officers, members, and the international unions in the goal-accomplishment process.

Regarding member perceptions of the locals' goals, it was found that many of the members believe their local unions should attempt to achieve a variety of goals both narrow and broad. Substantially more than half of the members who returned questionnaires indicate that their local unions should accomplish the following goals: higher wages, better working conditions, protection of workers from management, better health, pension, and insurance benefits, more job security, better seniority plan, equal rights for all workers, more members interested in the affairs of the local union, greater unity and strength in the local union, and more members educated about union affairs. Somewhat surprising is the finding that although higher wages are desired by a majority of the members, there is less support for the accomplishment of this goal than there is for most of the other goals included in the preceding list. This attitude contradicts the often heard view that American workers are interested primarily, sometimes exclusively, in the size of their paychecks.

Turning to those goals that received somewhat less support, between one-third and slightly more than one-half of the members in the samples believe their unions should strive for the following goals: longer vacations and more holidays, more social and recreational activities for workers, a better life for all people in the community, more support for the aims of the international, more organizing of unorganized plants, and more political action from members. With these all-encompassing goals, it is interesting to note that less than one-third of the members want more say in running the plant.

To forestall any inclination to generalize from these findings and thus maintain that the substantial numbers of members indicating support for broad, socially oriented goals (such as "a better life for all people in the community") are proof of the social consciousness of many union members, several comments are necessary. The various possible goals listed in the questionnaire might have suggested answers.[2] As a matter of fact, the members who were interviewed (and therefore had no answers suggested to them) seldom indicated that the goals were other than "protection," "wages," "working conditions," and various other answers associated with goals that would lead to greater organizational strength. This does not prove that all of those who were interviewed believe their unions have no other goals than protection, wages, and working conditions, since it is possible that people overlook certain aspects of a subject in a conversation for which there is no advance preparation. Nevertheless, it might be suggested that failure to mention the broader goals (e.g., more social and recreational activities, a better life for all people in the community, more support for the aims of the international, more organizing of unorganized plants) during the course of fairly lengthy interviews can be attributed to the lack of strong attachment to them.

Next, it is possible that many of those members indicating a preference for broader goals are merely rationalizing in order to reach a more socially acceptable position for the idea of unionism and in order to state a position that they believe university-oriented personnel might sanction. This is not an uncommon practice in American society. The businessman, for example, is not in business with the primary objective of making profits, but instead to serve the buying public. Similarly, the trade-unionist might maintain that the primary objectives of unions are to foster the broader social interests and welfare.

---

[2]However, the categories suggested in the questionnaire were distilled from information obtained from union members during the course of pretest procedures.

In either case, of course, failure to achieve an immediate or foreseeable personal economic gain would probably produce some type of realignment or change of the behavior of either the unions and their memberships or the business firm. While social welfare might be augmented by some individual or organizational behavior, it cannot be presumed that social welfare is the dominant motive for that behavior in the typical case. The incidental nature of the union's impact on social welfare as seen by many members who constituted our source of data can be identified in a partial quotation from an interview with one of the members:

> The job of the union is to take care of me. This is because I pay my dues and it's my money. The same goes for the other members of this local. Now, it's sometimes said that unions should help all workers. But it seems to me that they should help themselves just as I did. If they wanted a union, they could get one. They could get the same things we have. If you look at it another way, though, we do help all workers and the people in this town as well. When we get higher wages, we spend them, and this means somebody's income is going to go up. This means there's more profits and wages and everybody's better off than they were before.

Based on data acquired both by questionnaires and interviews, it seems reasonable to assert that the bulk of the membership supports the accomplishment of goals that are local in nature and that result in short-run returns to the members. Goals which, if accomplished would increase the organization's strength and hence increase the organization's capability to provide direct returns at some later time receive somewhat less membership support. While this appears to be an irrational attitude, some data were obtained that help to explain its existence.

First, approximately two-thirds of the members reported having been unemployed one or more times in their work careers. Periodic unemployment, particularly when it is followed by re-employment by another employer, might tend to produce the union member's attitude that it is quite risky, even useless, for him to make organizational commitments that will not pay off for some time. This would be true if the members believe it is possible that when the pay-off date comes they might be employed elsewhere.[3] Second, it is conceivable that many members may lack the necessary intellectual sophistication to identify the relationship between a broad goal (say, political action or organizational-membership drives) and their personal returns. Although not definitive, the educational backgrounds of the members who returned questionnaires are revealing in this respect.

TABLE 1

THE FORMAL EDUCATION OF THE MEMBERS

Highest Grade Achieved in School	Percentages of Total Number of Respondents
1–3 grades	3
4–7 grades	11
8 grades	21
9–11 grades	37
12 grades	24
13 grades or more	4
Total	100

[3]This possibility is worthy of considerably more intensive investigation than is mentioned for purposes of this study. During the period of time embracing this research, many of the workers organized in unions appear to be obsessed with the fear of displacement from their jobs. This obsession is fed by considerable attention given by the mass media, public officials, scholars, and others to the displacement effects of such phenomena as automation and technological change, foreign competition, and intense interindustry competition. Probably many members realize their unions are relatively powerless to counter such threats and, hence, become apathetic with respect to organizational affairs. It may be that the difference between the much heralded "good old days" of the thirties and forties and the problem-studded fifties and early sixties can be accounted for by the proposition that in earlier years members perceived their unions to be effective for dealing with their vital interests and problems, whereas today this is less and less so. Further, in the sixties government is underwriting some of the insecurity previously tackled by unions. Added reference will be made to this point in subsequent pages, although its complete elucidation requires the use of historical investigation and analysis.

Although there are many different ways to acquire insight into complex political, economic, and psychological relationships, it usually is assumed that education facilitates that process. In the case of members from the five local unions included in this study, less than one-half of them earned high school diplomas. In the absence of leadership focused on the more complex issues that confront them (more will be said about this later), it is reasonable for union members to direct their attention to the most obvious problems and solutions. The most obvious approaches are those that may be labeled "strictly local unionism," meaning by this unionism which is centered on local problems and issues. However, it should be noted that not all of the goals favored by the members are economic in character (in the sense that they can be easily, or even ultimately, quantified in units of dollars). The members did reveal interests in matters other than the size of their paychecks.

If union members are concerned with the accomplishment of goals which provide them with immediate and direct economic, psychological, and social returns, it would seem they would also believe the greatest barriers inhibiting success are those originating from employers and from the members' own unions. Most of the more desired goals seemingly require concessions from the employers if they are to be attained, and presumably, the effectiveness of the members' unions is the key to how much the employers can be expected to concede. In fact, certain of the goals most desired (such as "greater unity and strength in the local union") reflect the members' awareness of their reliance upon the union for representation to the employer in order to realize the other goals that depend on the employer's willingness to make concessions.

As expected, the union members seem to believe that the problems standing in the way of goal achievement originate from either the local or the company.

TABLE 2

THE PROBLEMS IDENTIFIED BY THE MEMBERS

Type of Local Union Problem	Percentages* of the Total Number of Respondents
Lack of interest by local union members	38
Hard management to deal with	35
Poor local union officers	27
No unity in the local union	22
A few bad local union members	22
Too little help from the international union	17
Bad public opinion about unions	12
Bad government laws concerning unions	7
I don't know what the problems are	7
Other	3

* The figures do not total 100 because each respondent could identify more than one problem.

However, it can be seen that most of the members were cognizant of problems that originate from within the local union, rather than from the outside, apart from those provided by management. Comparatively few members were concerned with public opinion or labor legislation at the time the data were collected. This attitude provides some explanation for the rather consistent refusal of union members to become involved with political and comunity-action programs: such programs are neither desired as goals in themselves nor viewed as problems which stand in the way of achieving goals which are both recognized and desired.

Although many of the members believe the union's problems are internal in origin, this by itself does not necessarily pinpoint the "true" problem. For example, a member might attribute the union's failure to accomplish certain goals to either the superior strength of the company or the weakness of the union, depending upon his inclinations and expectations. If he has been led to expect the union to accomplish certain objectives and it fails to achieve the expected, then the member is likely to charge the failure to the union, even though the situation might not permit anything other than failure. However, it is certain that most of the members believe the union's problems are local in both origin and nature.

Not unexpectedly, it was found that some of the categories of answers used in the questionnaire tended to conceal some of the complexity of the members' attitudes toward their unions' problems. One member who was interviewed said that most of the problems that exist in his local were caused by the members. He went on to say:

Some members slack down on their work. This slows down production so that some companies don't have enough money to do some of the things the union wants. This is because some members have the idea "the world owes me a living." They have no interests or don't like their jobs.

This comment points out interaction between the members and the company that results in a problem: the company is unable to meet the union's demands because of the low productivity of some of the members. In turn, the low productivity of some of the members is attributed to their own unsuitable attitudes, as judged by other members. Quite frequently, the members who were interviewed could be placed in either of two categories: those who are prounion and anti-employer in the sense that they favored harassing the employer by compelling him to accept inefficient, arbitrary production methods and job rules; and those who are prounion but more or less neutral with respect to the employer in the sense that they favored the more efficient job rules and production methods that would lead to greater earnings and could thus constitute the basis for an improved labor agreement via collective bargaining. The members who have anti-employer attitudes are antagonistic and rebellious toward the employer and see their union memberships as means of protection as they give vent to these attitudes. Those who are neutral with regard to the employer recognize the co-operative nature of the relationship between labor and management necessary to produce income in capitalistic business enterprises but nevertheless believe it is necessary to compete with the company for the distribution of that income. Considerable conflict exists between members holding these opposed attitudes.

It must be recognized that the members' identification of organizational problems is not necessarily the outcome of an objective interpretation of the goals and reasons for the failure to achieve them. One member who was interviewed maintained the local president was the big problem. He said:

The president is a company man. If you call him at his home with a problem, he says, "I'll handle it later." He didn't show up at the picket line during the last strike. He just sat around talking with management. He doesn't file grievances for the men. . . nor is he outwardly friendly with the men in the shop.

Somewhat by chance, the interviewer found out later that this particular member had been one of the president's most ardent supporters—until one day when the member left his machine to speak to the president about a personal matter and was told "this isn't the time or place for you to talk to me about that." Since that time, relations between the two had become more and more hostile.

Although some 27 per cent of the members returning questionnaires believe abilities or devotion of their officers constitute problems, not all of this can be attributed to personality problems. There is reason to believe that the performances of the union officers are compared to the performances of their management counterparts and suffer by the comparison. Many times the local officers, professionally untrained, are required to argue their cases with such people as engineers, lawyers, and accountants. Unless they have the benefit of an airtight case or professional counsel, their chances of winning may be remote. Sometimes this state of affairs was explicitly recognized by the members. During an interview, one said, "Our president isn't very good, although he's the best we got." Another member observed, "Our president is a nice guy, but it takes more than a nice guy to stand up to professionals."

However, the general picture remains unchanged: the members perceive both their goals and problems to be local and immediate. This same kind of outlook was found when the members were asked to identify the means that the union had for dealing with its problems. Almost all of the members who were interviewed indicated that the only available means were such things as "bargaining," "compromising with management," "threatening to strike," "strike," or "talking it over with management." The same thing was found in the data collected through the use of questionnaires.

At the same time, most of the members realize that the strength of the local union depends upon the willingness of the members to back the union. They noted that meeting attendance was useful for demonstrating strength to the company. In general, they recognize that in the end, the real strength of the union amounts to its ability to strike. The strength of the union ultimately is its membership, they said. Essentially, however, most of the members are inclined to desire moderate, rather than militant, means of dealing with the company. This is readily visible from the data obtained by the questionnaires.

TABLE 3

MEANS FOR ACCOMPLISHING THE UNION'S GOALS
THAT WERE IDENTIFIED BY THE MEMBERS

Means Preferred by the Respondents	Percentages of Total Number of Respondents
Just bargain or talk it over with management..	29
Get more unity from local union members and put pressure on management......................	24
Compromise with management........................	16
Make demands and threaten to strike..............	11
Strike	8
I don't know the best way..............................	7
Other	3
Use political action	2
None of these methods is proper......................	1
Total	101*

* This total is not 100 because of rounding.

Again it can be seen that almost none of the members believes political action is an effective way to accomplish union goals.

It should be noted that none of the answers in the preceding table contains any reference to the international union as a means of accomplishing union goals. No such answers were included in the questionnaire since the international union was not mentioned in this capacity by any of the members who were interviewed during the pretest phase of the study. This omission is important in itself. It reinforces the conception of the members' attitudes toward unionism as a strictly local system of relationships which have some continuity over time. This is not to say that the members conceive no role whatsoever for the international union; as will be shown later, however, the members' concept of the international's role is extremely limited.

Attention is directed next to the members' expectations regarding the organizational roles of the members, the local officers, and the international union. First, however, several preliminary comments are in order.

Unions in America, structurally, are democratic organizations. Whether unions choose to use political, social, or economic means on narrow or broad fronts, their strength is derived from the individual members. Union power may be manifested in a variety of ways, including strikes, strike threats that are realistic in appearance, political action, and various social pressures. In each of these, the efficiency in their application depends upon the individual member's willingness to do something: withhold his labor from the employer, attend union meetings and make his dissatisfactions obvious to all interested observers, engage in political campaigns (including casting his own ballot), and act to influence public opinion either individually or collectively by providing funds and personal labor to be used for "educational" programs. Despite frequent allegations to the contrary, the treasuries of separate local or autonomous international unions are incapable of sustaining pure "money power" efforts to accomplish union goals.[4] Thus far in the development of American unionism, no substitute for the individual efforts of unionists has appeared. This, along with the formally democratic features of union organizations, should tend to produce organizational roles of certain types.

Democratic operations require the body of members to determine the basic policies of the organization. In such determination of policies, they would be advised by "experts" —local union officers and various elements in the international union hierarchy. In turn, the local union officers and

---

[4]According to Alexander Heard, "the conclusion seems inescapable that labor money in politics from all sources pays a much smaller share of the nation's campaign-connected costs than union members constitute of the population of voting age" (see *The Costs of Democracy* [Garden City, N.Y.: Anchor books, 1962], p. 179).

the international union hierarchy would be responsible for the implementation of basic policy. Maintenance of organizational strength, however, calls for extensive membership participation in organizational affairs. This serves the functions of communications, co-ordination, and demonstration of strength. If both these organizational prerequisites (basic policy determination and maintenance of organizational strength) are recognized by the members, they will perceive, in addition, continually active organizational roles for themselves and union officers. Let us turn now to the roles as they actually are perceived by the members.

A large majority of the members (75 per cent) believed they should participate in the affairs of the local union. Generally, the word "participation" was used by them to include such activities as attending meetings, taking part in discussions of local business, voting, co-operating with stewards, and the like. Furthermore, roughly two-thirds to three-fourths of the members said they believed their local officers expected these things from them. Their actual performance was another matter, however, as evidenced by the following data obtained from those members returning questionnaires:

1. Fifty-eight per cent of the members attended only one-quarter or fewer of the regular meetings the preceding year.

2. Fifty-seven per cent of the members attended only one-third or fewer of the special meetings in the preceding year.

3. Eighty-nine per cent of the members were not when interviewed nor had ever served on union committees.

4. Eighty-seven per cent of the members were not when interviewed nor had ever served as union officers.

Further, approximately one-third of the members attended no meetings at all in the preceding year. On the other hand, 70 per cent of the members said they had voted in the last election of local officers.

Frequently it is claimed that although members may fail to participate in any measurable way, the level of "participation" may yet be high. One such method of participation would be the maintenance of the member–local union relationship through the medium of the stewards or other active members. While this may be true insofar as communications are concerned, it is hardly plausible that certain other functions can be served adequately in this way. To illustrate this with reference to one function which seemingly has considerable relevance for most local unions, we may consider the demonstration of power function.

Power demonstrations, in this case the demonstration of membership unity in dissatisfaction, have the purpose of serving notice on the employer of the possibility of a work stoppage or other penalty, presently or in the future, if certain conditions are not met. If the demonstration is successful (that is, obvious), the employer can react with some certainty as to possible implications following his reaction. In turn, the union can be more confident that the employer's reaction was conditioned by knowledge of the actual risk involved. While this state of affairs does not eliminate uncertainty and the consequent necessity for a certain amount of bluffing, it does remove much of the threat which would be presented by either of the parties acting in complete ignorance of possible retaliations. The argument, then, is that successful power demonstrations reduce the possibility that the union will have to employ its ultimate weapon, the strike, in cases where its only usefulness is proving to the employer that the members really do want something badly enough to strike. Only overt, obvious membership participation will satisfy the conditions imposed by the need to demonstrate dissatisfaction and unity.

Elsewhere it will be claimed that "informal participation" is inefficient from other points of view as well. Whatever the effect of formal participation may be upon the presence or absence of democracy in local unions, our belief is that participation in the formal sense is necessary for continuing organizational strength, as well as for facilitating the process of leadership. Such participation was clearly lacking in the five local unions described here.

Although the members said their role was to participate in the affairs of the local union, for the most part they failed to act in this capacity. The so-called "actives" identifiable in this study were too small a group to be consistently representative of the membership attitudes in general. At least it may be said that no formal or observable informal means existed to insure even minimally that the small group of actives was representative. Thus, the typical member really expects either the small group of "actives" (including the local officers), or the international union to provide the day-to-day support for local union operations.

Turning to member expectations for the international, it was found that one-half or more of the members returning questionnaires believed the international should provide help when requested by the local union, keep the local informed, and offer advice and suggestions.

TABLE 4

LOCAL UNION MEMBERS' EXPECTATIONS
FOR THE INTERNATIONAL UNION

What Members Believe Is Expected From International Union	Percentages of Total Number of Respondents
To help out when requested by the local	27
To keep the local informed	24
To offer advice and suggestions about how the local should be run	22
To organize unorganized plants in the industry	16
To keep the local "in line" by telling it what to do	7
I don't know what the local expects	4
Total	100

All in all, the members seemed to picture the international's role as that of providing certain services that would facilitate local union operations. These data and more detailed information acquired during the interviews confirm that the members' concept of unionism is strictly local unionism, rather than movement or widespread organizational unionism. For example, less than one-half of the members who returned questionnaires expected the international to organize unorganized plants in the industry even after this answer was suggested to them. Almost none of those interviewed volunteered this expectation. Moreover, the interviews revealed that the most commonly desired service from the international was the provision of strike benefits. Other services desired were technical advice and guidance, particularly in such fields as engineering and law. Political and community-action programs, so much desired by higher echelons within unions, aroused little membership approval, enthusiasm, or support.

If the international union does not play a vital, continuing role in the members' concept of unionism, then the local officers represent the only remaining possibility for sustaining the local operation and providing leadership. In fact, the interviews and questionnaires both revealed the members' reliance on the officers' performances for the day-to-day organizational operations.

The local officers are expected to win grievances, to keep the members informed, to protect union members, and to be "fair and honest" with the members and the company. It might be pointed out that information acquired during the interviews indicated that many members used the term "protection" to refer to job and wage security. Therefore, it seems reasonable to conclude that most of the members probably depended upon the officers to accomplish those goals which, logically, are the most important local union goals. Moreover, our data revealed that most of the members apparently did not believe the officers should be subjected to detailed direction by the members.

TABLE 5

RESPONDENT'S EXPECTATIONS FOR THEIR LOCAL OFFICERS

What Members Expect Most From Their Local Officers	Percentages of Total Number of Respondents
To be honest and fair with local union members	14
To be honest and fair with management	13
To fight to win grievances	11
To keep the local union members informed	11
To protect all the local union members all the time	11
To run a democratic union meeting	8
To be tough bargainers with management	7
To be leaders in the community	6
To do what local union members say	5
To compromise with management	5
To get all they can out of management	4
No strikes	4
Total	99*

* This total is not 100 because of rounding.

Most of the members again demonstrated their disinclination for broad-gauge unionism in answering the question about their expectations for local union officers. Considerably less than a majority said they expect their officers "to be leaders in the community."

The conclusion is inescapable: even though most members seem to believe that continuous membership participation is essential for the success of local union endeavors, they delegate the responsibility for local union operations to the local officers and, perhaps, a minority of other active members.

Briefly summarized, the typical member's conception of unionism in the five locals studied here is as follows:

1. It is unionism that is almost completely limited to matters that arise between the employer and the members of the local union.

2. It is unionism that, consequently, should attempt to deal with problems originating either from the employer or the local union's inability to deal with the employer.

3. It is unionism that deals with its problems primarily with local union resources (particularly work stoppages or threatened stoppages) applied either against the company or in strengthening the union.

4. It is unionism that relies heavily and continually on the local union officers, heavily but probably not continually on most members, and somewhat continually but least heavily on the international union hierarchy.

From this we may conclude tentatively that most union members in our samples cannot realistically be described as belonging to a single local union group: if they are described as organization members, this description applies only to the local organization, rather than the local *and* the international as interrelated components of one unit. However, this conclusion requires additional reinforcement; we shall return to it later.

Satisfactions Members Get From Unionism

IT IS CLEAR by now that most of the members of the five local unions that are the subjects of this study are not members of the "union movement" in terms of the attitudes which reveal their concept of unionism. "Movement" is a term usually reserved for the collective efforts of people joined together by the common desire to accomplish some more or less fundamental, far-reaching social changes. In contrast to this, the majority of members of these local unions are motivated only toward solution of local situations and problems.

But this raises a significant question: if these local unions are not part of a social movement or part of a group, do they at least constitute organizations? This question derives its importance from the nature of this study of union *leadership*. As noted above, one prerequisite for the emergence of leadership is the existence of a group or organization.

A group or organization is composed of people who have something in common. Usually they have common interests which, if provided for, result in supplying some kind of satisfactions to the individual. Sometimes these satisfactions are derived from the very existence of the group or organization. Examples of satisfactions of this kind might be companionship, friendship, or prestige. In contrast with this, satisfactions may also be derived from sources external to the group or organization itself, stemming from the efforts of the individuals. In either case, however, the cohesive force holding the unit together is the actual or potential acquisition of satisfaction.

While trade-unions may exhibit some of the characteristics associated with groups, we have already shown it is likely that they will tend to have more characteristics of organizations. In turn, if they are seeking to accomplish fundamental social changes, they may blend into a social movement. The attitudes that would warrant the general use of the terms group and social movement were not found among the majority of the union members studied here.

The question is, then, how much organization quality is demonstrated by the members of the five locals? The attitudes described above are not conducive to a definite answer. We need to know more about what induces union members to act cohesively, even if only infrequently. Is it because the member is getting group satisfactions? Is he acting ritualistically? Is he acting irrationally? Fully cognizant of the difficulty of answering such questions with assurance, we believed the best possibility was to attempt determination of the satisfactions obtained by the union members from their union membership. Knowledge of the nature of the satisfactions was expected to provide some clue regarding the nature of the union members' organizational characteristics. Table 6 shows the satisfactions members reported as derived from union membership.

TABLE 6

Satisfactions Members Get from Their Unions

Types of Satisfactions	Percentages of Total Number of Respondents
A feeling of security	19
Higher wages and better working conditions	17
Having good friends who are union brothers	12
Feeling I am part of an important group	10
Feeling I can help other members through the union	10
Feeling I have more say about wages and conditions in the plant	10
Feeling that I learn from being part of a union	10
A feeling of protection from the boss	7
I don't get any satisfactions from the union	2
I don't know what satisfaction I get from the union	2
Other	1
Total	100

First of all, a few members get no satisfactions at all from their union; a few more don't know for sure what satisfactions they do obtain. Presumably, these members do not constitute a part of the union when it is viewed as an organization. However, most members do report satisfactions and thus probably are part of the union organization. But it is important to consider the differences between the varying satisfactions they receive. On the one hand, there are those satisfactions that originate from within the union itself: "satisfaction from feeling I am part of an important group"; "satisfaction from having good friends who are union brothers"; "satisfaction from feeling I can help other members through the union"; "satisfaction from feeling I learn from being part of the union." Other satisfactions originate from the union's external accomplishment: "satisfaction from a feeling of security"; "satisfaction from higher wages and working conditions." It can be seen that most members receive satisfactions from the union's external accomplishments.

The point is that it is likely that those members who receive satisfactions from within the union itself will be more conscious of their mutual rights and responsibilities and will perceive these over a much wider range of activities than the members receiving only the kinds of satisfactions that must be acquired from outside the organization. To illustrate (although this cannot be precisely measured), those members who were interviewed and said that they receive satisfactions from within the organization itself also seem to be more active, less critical of their officers, and perceive a broader type of unionism. However, additional work is necessary to verify the existence of this relationship. The data concerning satisfactions seem to warrant the suggestion that those union members either receiving no satisfactions or unable to identify their satisfactions and those members receiving only "satisfaction from feeling of security" and "satisfaction from higher wages and better working conditions" are marginal organization members or are not organization members at all. Those people may desire some of the economic and psychological benefits of unionism, but they are unable or unwilling to accept responsibility to the organization in return, except in a minimal sense. They may unwillingly or willingly man the picket lines on occasion; they also pay their dues; many of them will vote in union elections, although they probably vote against, rather than for, the candidates for office, since their limited participation must fail to produce knowledge of alternative policies and administrative patterns. Such members, individualistically oriented most of the time, are conscious of the union and its responsibility to them as individuals, particularly when they are beset by personal difficulties and dissatisfactions. Most of them are not anti-union; instead, they regard the union in something like the manner most people regard insurance policies—to be used in emergencies. In the judgment of the writer, such members as these probably constitute majorities of the memberships of the five local unions.

Apparently, therefore, it is inappropriate to conceptualize all local union members as members of organizations, as we are using the term. Groups may, and do, exist within such organizations, but they do not include the whole membership. It is likely, for example, that most of the more active union members constitute some sort of group within each local union. Or the more active members may constitute two or more groups, if factionalism or organized opposition is present in the situation. However, since most members appear to be outside any union groups, ultimate political control rests with those who perceive the least responsibility to unions and also derive the least satisfactions from their membership. More important yet for our purposes, large numbers of the members of the five locals included in our study possess characteristics of such nature as to complicate attempted leader behavior. Moreover, there are certain additional problems which compound the difficulty; these are associated with the communications structures in the five locals.

Communications in Local Unions

WHILE the leadership context in local unions is composed partially of member attitudes as those described above, it also is affected by the formal and informal means of communications within these organizations. In fact, there is always the likelihood of interdependence between the formation of attitudes and internal communications. Just as important, however, is the dependence of effective leadership on the ability to transmit and receive information. Thus, we turn next to communications in the five unions studied.

We found no evidence of organized, informal, and local-wide communications systems in any of the five local unions. By "organized informal communications systems" we mean those systems which exist on a dependable and continuing basis, although they are not formally provided for by union constitutions or bylaws. Such systems could amount to regular dissemination of news and opinions about union affairs from, say, highly active members to less active members; the system could consist of stewards serving as the key links in the communication process between the members and the top local union officers. Instead, we found traces of informal systems existing within subgroups of members and, occasionally, between subgroups and one or several officers. None of these systems, however, appears to embrace a large segment, or large segments, of the members. Thus, the unions apparently must depend upon the formal communications (such as meeting attendance, bulletin board notices, and mailed literature) and imperfectly functioning informal systems (such as talking with stewards, local officers, and other members).

In order to determine the comparative importance of a number of different means of communications, the questionnaires contained the following questions:

1. What are your chief sources of news about union affairs?

2. How do you find out what your local officers want your local to do?

3. How do you find out what your international wants the local to do?

Turning first to the members' chief sources of news about union affairs, it is apparent that no single source is thought to be primary by a large majority of members. Instead, the members appear to rely upon a combination of sources, of which the most important seems to be talking with other members and stewards. Next in importance are bulletin board notices and attending local meetings.

TABLE 7

CHIEF SOURCES OF NEWS ABOUT UNION AFFAIRS

Members' Chief Sources of News	Percentages of Total Number of Respondents
Talking with other union members	23
Talking with stewards	19
Reading the bulletin board	18
Attending local union meetings	16
Reading notices and reports that come in the mail	12
Talking with top local union officers	10
I have no chief source of news	1
Other	1
Total	100

Conversations with local officers and mailed notices and reports are not regarded highly as sources of information about union affairs.

Similar patterns emerge from the members' response to the question: "How do you find out what your local officers want the local to do?" Most members find out their officers' views about union affairs from other union members and stewards. Quite a few also find out through written materials, attending union meetings, and asking the officers directly.

TABLE 8

Chief Sources of Information about Officers' Views

Members' Sources of Information	Percentages of Total Number of Respondents
Other union members	25
The steward	22
Reading notices and bulletins	14
Asking the top local union officers	14
Listening to the top officers	8
Attending union meetings	7
Don't know what the officers think	7
Other	2
Total	99*

* This total is not 100 because of rounding.

With respect to securing information about the international union's desires for the local, a large proportion of members again say they depend on other union members. Apparently the stewards and the union paper are also information sources for quite a few members. Somewhat fewer members get their information from the meetings and other sources listed in the questionnaires.

Several different points emerge from these data. The members principally depend on other union members for sources of union news in general, as well as for information about their local officers' and international union's views. Meetings, direct contacts with union officers other than stewards, and printed materials are of secondary importance. (The secondary ranking of meetings could have been predicted from data dealing with meeting attendance.) This means that the locals are heavily dependent upon comparatively inefficient means of communication. This inefficiency stems from two basic limitations. First, the information sources reported by most

TABLE 9

MEMBERS' CHIEF SOURCES OF INFORMATION ABOUT
THE INTERNATIONAL UNION'S VIEWS

Members' Sources of Information	Percentages of Total Number of Respondents
Other union members	21
Reading the union paper	19
The steward	17
Attending union meetings	16
Asking the top union officers	8
Don't know what the international union thinks	8
Listening to the top officers	7
The international representative	3
Other	1
Total	100

members can usually reach only relatively small numbers of people at any one time. Second, these sources are more likely to distort information in the process of its transmission. Such distortion is not necessarily deliberate. Distortion may occur because of the difficulties of understanding and remembering what has been heard; it may also occur because different words have different meanings for different people. These are but a few of the attendant difficulties associated with mouth-to-mouth communications.

Next, it is apparent that although almost none of the members said they have no chief sources of information about union affairs, more of the members confessed to being without information as to their officers' and the international's views. This may mean that the members are not interested in these views, or that they are interested but lack the means to find out what the views are. In any event, it is suggested that this is another indication of the inefficiency inherent in the communications systems in these locals.

The complete de-emphasis of means to bring original sources into direct contact with intended recipients necessitates the transmission of information through comparatively slow, inaccurate, and discontinuous procedures. Furthermore, it is well known that many members who do attend meetings or make personal contacts with their officers do so only when they are confronted with personal or small-group problems. Thus, such communications as are accomplished, through whatever means as are employed, are likely to be those associated with specific job and shop problems.

It must be concluded on the basis of everything known about these five locals that no continuous and widely inclusive communications channels are functioning. That they may function on some occasion, such as during negotiations and stoppages, is not denied; they do not exist on a day-to-day basis. Further, it is likely that when they do exist, it is at the discretion of the members, rather than the officers.

Since members apparently lack movement, group, and in some cases even organization characteristics, a barrier is created to the emergence of leadership. The problem is compounded by what appears to be a lack of central, continuous access to the membership. This problem is in no way ameliorated by crisis-motivated members who flock to the halls from time to time and then to the picket line. At the same time, it must be recognized that the apparent non-existence of functioning local-wide communications systems is consistent with the apparent non-existence of local-wide group and organization attitudes and expectations previously described.

Differences among the Locals

THUS FAR, primary consideration has been given to patterns of attitudes and behavior identifiable in the study of union members without regard to differences among members from different local unions. While this approach is appropriate for understanding the general environment within which the union leader must function, for some purposes it is useful to focus attention on such differences as do exist. It will be demonstrated in subsequent chapters that the extent and quality of leadership are variable among the five locals. While cause and effect cannot be precisely isolated, it appears that the variation is associated with a number of observable differences among the locals. That is, the locals with larger numbers of followers, group or organization members, also seem to be the ones whose top local officers' behavior more nearly conforms to the leadership criteria established in Chapter I. Hence, although the differences among the members of the various locals are not extensive, they do have implications for the status of local union leadership.

One of the most obvious differences among the five locals is that local A has significantly more members who are active than the other four. Even though the definition of active may be elusive, it seems reasonable to assume that locals, for example, that have higher proportions of their members who attend regular and special meetings, vote, and are well informed have more actives than those who do not. More members of local A than the members of other locals attend meetings, vote in elections, serve on committees, run for offices, and report that they know the local's and international's positions on union matters. Moreover, examination of these and other data suggest forcefully the conclusion that local A possesses more organizational characteristics than the other four, and furthermore, that local A possesses more union movement characteristics than the others. This is not to say that local A is a perfect example of a group, organization, or movement union. It is not. But compared to the other four locals, it has more members with group, organization, and movement characteristics.

The information that local A has more active members and, concomitantly, better informed members, leads directly to the conclusion that this local, more than the others, possesses a structure which is made up of mutually perceived rights and responsibilities. In turn, the combination of structure and more effective communications channels supports the suggestion that local A is probably more cohesive than the other four. That is, there is a fairly high probability that local A has more unity, vigor, and success as far as its members are concerned than the other four locals. As a matter of fact, our own judgment, based on both the acquired objective evidence and impressions formed over the course of the study, is that local A conforms more nearly than the others to the industrial-democracy union—the union in which democratic methods are operable within the organization, and democratic attitudes are instrumental in shaping the organization's goals and methods of dealing with external parties. It also is more successful from its members' points of view.

In contrast to local A, local D has many more members who are uninformed, generally inactive, and uninterested in their union. At the same time, the recent history of local D is marked by apparently baseless factionalism, wildcat strikes, and other signs of disorganization. On one occasion at least, the wildcat strike was as much a demonstration against the union as against the company and, as closely as can be judged, destroyed the union's ability to accomplish any goals for some period of time. More of the members of this local than the others appear to be self-oriented to the point where this orientation becomes self-defeating. Thus, local D possesses almost none of the group, organization, or movement characteristics.

One of the locals standing somewhere between local D and local A in terms of cohesiveness and effectiveness (again judging this from the members' point of view) is local C.

This local is somewhat distinct for another reason. Whereas the other locals almost exclusively depend upon the formal structures (the structures specified in their constitutions and bylaws) for the conduct of union business and meet with varying degrees of success, the information obtained from the members of local C indicates the existence of a more highly developed informal structure in that union. In the absence of meeting attendance, several of the local-wide officers in local C use personal contacts with the members, both in and out of the meeting hall and shop, in order to communicate facts and ideas about union business. Similarly, the stewards in this local are employed somewhat more frequently as communications channels than in the other locals. Although an informal structure built upon personal contacts may be the only possibility for improved communications and organizational cohesion in this local, there are some indications that this approach is of limited usefulness (as suggested above). In the first place, the informal structure did not include all of the members of the local, as evidenced by a fairly large group of members who knew little or nothing of current local affairs. Next, some of the members we believe are included in the informal structure apparently received erroneous information which left them misinformed about seemingly important union affairs. There is reason to believe this is the consequence of passing information by word of mouth. Finally, the members' dependence upon stewards and officers as links to the organization increases the difficulties of performing those roles by personalizing the officer-member relationships to the point where it is difficult to place some items into the information stream because of the personal nature of some issues. Also, and possibly even more important, union officers who must function in this capacity find that heavy, inefficient demands consequently are made upon the time they have available to attend to union affairs.

For the most part, the successful operation of a continuous, local-wide, informal structure requires unusually gifted and energetic officers, stewards, and active members. They must be capable of thoroughly understanding, summarizing, rephrasing, and repeating ideas, attitudes, opinions, and facts without regard for their personal preferences and inclinations. Unfortunately, the officers of local C, despite their sincere efforts, lack these capabilities. It must be expected that the degree of training and education that would be required for the maintenance of an effective informal structure, suitable for substituting for the formal structure, would be so extensive as to preclude its feasibility in the usual case. This is especially so, given the periodic replacement of local-wide officers and stewards due to elections. The comparison of the more highly structured local A with the more informal organization of local C points out, once again, the local union's need for simple, efficient mechanisms (such as regular meetings) in order to achieve organizational strength and efficiency.

Summary and Conclusions

IF WE VIEW the local union memberships as part of the environment within which the leadership process must emerge and develop, it must be concluded that the environment is hostile. Most of the members probably demand certain job or shop services in response to individual and small-group problems and dissatisfactions. The members expect the services to be provided by the officers, except when there is need for occasional membership-wide threats or demonstrations of force. Moreover, it is probable that the officers are evaluated primarily by their success in providing personal and small-group services. Even their collective bargaining functions may be evaluated in this manner, the bargaining probably is evaluated in terms of its impact upon individuals and small groups, rather than its implications for the entire local membership, let alone the international organization. In this context, the problem is compounded by the limitations of local-wide communications channels. Attempts to change membership attitudes and expectations through the exercise of persuasion seemingly would lack an effective medium for their transmission.

The evaluation above is by no means true of all members in the local unions. Some members are willing to accept responsibilities to the organization on a continual basis, but it appears that they are a minority. Thus, they are incapable of providing the political defense for an officer who attempts to depart from the pattern of strictly limited, personal-service, insurance unionism. Therefore, it seems to be most useful to emphasize the qualities, characteristics, and implications of the majorities, since they loom as the critical elements in the membership as far as leadership problems are concerned.

The foregoing description leads to the conclusion that the practice of leadership may be difficult in the five local unions. Certainly there is a great leadership challenge.

4. Local Union Officers as Leaders: A Description and Evaluation

Characteristics of the Officers

ONE OF THE OBJECTIVES of the present work is to describe and evaluate systematically the practice of leadership in local unions. In previous chapters, we have discussed the union organizations and membership characteristics which constitute the context for leadership. With this background, we now turn to a description of activities of local union officers and an evaluation of that activity against the formal criteria of leadership outlined in Chapter I.

The presidents and executive boards of the five local unions of the study provided the focus for our assessment of leadership. This sample of officers included, in addition to the presidents, all the top elected officials of each local, including vice-presidents, secretaries, and treasurers. The number of officers included from each local varied between six and nine, with the combined total in the whole sample numbering forty-one.[1] As a group, these officials constituted the most select, active, interested, and committed members of their locals, members from whom leadership acts most logically could have been expected.

---

[1] Differences among locals in the number of officers studied occurred because the number of officers on the executive board of a local union varies according to the bylaws of the local and the number of board vacancies which may exist.

In age, the officers represented a range from the early twenties to past sixty, with a slightly greater number in their forties than in any other age group. The median number of years of education in the group was ten, and the median number of years in their present union offices was three to four. On the whole, the officers had been union members of long standing, the preponderant majority having belonged for ten or more years. Five of the group were women.

Information concerning the behavior of the officers was obtained chiefly through interviews with the officers themselves. Every effort was made to use questions and procedures which would provide as complete, objective, and accurate a description of the officers' behavior as possible, short of directly observing them in the actual discharge of their duties. Direct observation would have been desirable but was judged impractical, considering that many duties of local union officers are quite likely to be performed at odd hours, both on and off the job, and both night and day. In many instances, it was possible to achieve substantial verification of the information obtained in the interviews by comparing the officers' reports of their activities to reports made by local union members and international representatives. In the judgment of the writers, the data to be presented in this chapter constitute an accurate picture of the behavior of the officers of the sample. There is no reason to believe that the officers provided us anything but straightforward accounts of their activities, attitudes, and beliefs.

Behavior of Officers in Office

THE DISCUSSION which follows includes descriptions of the amounts of time local unions officers spend on union affairs, activities in which they engage, activities they consider most important, and what they feel their union duties are and should be. The objective is a broad characterization of leadership orientation and practice in the officer group.

The amount of time per week an officer spends on union business is an integral part of his approach to union office. Contrary to what certain past studies[2] had suggested we might expect to find, a large majority of our sample seemed not to spend an exorbitant amount of time on union affairs. Twenty-eight officers, or two-thirds of the total sample, reported spending nine or fewer hours on union business in an average week, while only six officers of the sample reported spending as many as twenty or more hours per week. There was some tendency to spend more hours on union affairs in especially busy weeks. In reply to a question concerning the most hours spent on union business in any one week within the past three months, twenty-four officers, or three-fifths of the sample, reported having spent ten or more hours in such a week. The amount of time spent even in a busy week does not seem unduly great, however. The findings which indicate an increase in the number of hours officers spend in a busy, as compared to an average, week are largely a function of more officers spending ten to nineteen hours in a busy week and a lesser number spending only nine or fewer. It is pertinent to note that for some officers a portion of time spent on union affairs represents time away from the job, for which compensation from the union is received. The amount of personal time spent on union business thus amounts to something, perhaps considerably, less than even the above figures indicate.

Findings concerning officers' expenditures of time on union business varied little from local to local. There was only a limited tendency for time spent to be related to the amount of help available from the international representative, and

---

[2]Leonard R. Sayles and George Strauss, *The Local Union: Its Place in the Industrial Plant* (New York: Harper and Bros., 1953); Alvin W. Gouldner, "Attitudes of 'Progressive' Trade Union Leaders," *American Journal of Sociology*, LII (1947), 389-92.

this tendency was in a direction opposite to that which seems most logical—i.e., for less time to be spent by officers who receive much help. A slightly greater amount of time on union affairs apparently was spent by the officers of A and B, two locals from an international which provided easily obtained services. Amounts of time spent on union affairs seem unlikely to be determined by any one factor but, rather, by a combination of factors, including the type of office held, energy level of the officer, officer's orientation to responsibilities, and demands of the immediate situation.

TABLE 10

AMOUNTS OF TIME OFFICERS SPEND ON UNION DUTIES

Average Number of Hours Reported Spent per Week	Number of Officers* (Total N-41)	Most Hours Reported Spent in Any One Week in Past Three Months	Number of Officers* (N-40) †
0–9	28	0–9	16
10–19	7	10–19	14
20–29	4	20–29	3
30–39	2	30–39	5
40–49	....	40–49	1
50 or more	....	50 or more	1

* Percentages were not used due to relatively small size of total sample.
† One officer of the total sample of 41 did not respond to the question.

Local union presidents spent slightly more hours on union affairs than lesser officers. While the presidents of B and E fit the general tendency of the total sample by reporting spending nine or fewer hours on union business in an average week, the presidents of A and D spent ten to nineteen hours and the president of C twenty to twenty-nine hours. The difference between the presidents and other officers is more apparent in hours spent in a busy week. The president of C reported spending forty to forty-nine hours in a recent heavy week, the president of A thirty to thirty-nine, and the president of D twenty to twenty-nine. Two of these, the presidents of A and C, reported that the least number of hours per week they *ever* spent on union business was ten to nineteen. In contrast to this rather heavy commitment of time, the president of E reported spending nine or fewer hours on union business even in his busiest week, and the president of B, ten to nineteen hours in his busiest week.

Despite the variation, it seems clear that presidents spend more time on union business than other local officers. However, even the presidents do not seem extraordinarily burdened with union business in the average week, considering that for most of them, a portion of the time spent on union business would otherwise be spent on the job. In another sense, since none of the presidents studied was paid, even the moderate commitment of time reported represents an important dedication to union responsibilities. It is also possible that time spent in personal reflection about decisions and possible actions does not show up in our findings. Nonetheless, the over-all picture which emerges does not seem to support the image sometimes painted of the energetic and tireless, but over-worked and harried, local union official who spends long tedious hours at union business.

Although information concerning the amounts of time officers spend on union affairs is helpful in describing their behavior in office, knowledge of specific activities in which they engage is more important in characterizing and evaluating leadership practices.

Interview questions were used to collect and verify information concerning specific activities local union officers perform in carrying out their duties. One question required the officers to judge which of their union activities takes the most time; another elicited a judgment concerning which of their activities the officers considered most important; a third, and less direct type of question, required the officers to explain why much time is spent on union affairs in certain weeks, and much less in others. Responses to these questions indicated that the local union officers spent their time primarily in attending to routine administrative matters, such as record-keeping, and in handling specific problems of members as they arise, such as grievances. For example, when asked to indicate types of union business which were the most time-consuming, of the forty-one officers interviewed, eighteen indicated that grievances took much time; thirteen reported attending meetings; and ten indicated preparation and presentation of records. The only other activity mentioned as time-consuming by as many as five or more officers was negotiating the contract, mentioned by eight.

TABLE 11

ACTIVITIES WHICH OFFICERS REPORT REQUIRE MOST TIME

Type of Activity Reported	Number of Officers (Total N-41)*
Dealing with grievances	18
Attending the local's meetings	13
Preparation and presentation of records	10
Negotiating the contract	8
Meeting with the executive board	4
Correspondence	3
Audits	3
Eight additional miscellaneous activities reported	11

* The number of officers totals more than 41, since more than one activity could be reported.

Although, as might be expected, the specific routine activity which demanded most time varied somewhat with the office (such as treasurers spending more time with audits), the general pattern was quite consistent for all offices represented in the sample. Of eighteen time-consuming activities reported by the five presidents, twelve involved dealing with grievances or attending meetings. Four of the five presidents indicated that dealing with grievances was the single most time-consuming activity of their office. In fact, the president of D reported that as much as 80 per cent of his time spent on union business was taken up with grievances. The president of C put it this way:

The grievance procedure takes the most of my time. I'm talking about the grievances that I handle after working hours, too. Because usually the stewards will come in at quitting time, and maybe they can't handle it—maybe they don't quite know what it is. So they want to know whether the person has a grievance, has the right to file a grievance. I'd say the grievance procedure comes first all the time, even of the work I do at home.

It all involves time. . . . Maybe somebody has a grievance. If you are chairman of the meeting, you have to have the papers ready to explain it to him, or . . . where a grievance pertains to a department, one section might be satisfied with the answer and the other section isn't. Then you might have to prepare a brief to show both parties what action was taken.

The same officer mentioned a related but slightly different type of time-consuming activity:

A lot of times dealing with the company takes time. Maybe they come up with a new rule; it's not really a grievance where a member would protest. But they post it and say it is going to be in effect in three days' time. And we feel it is unfair. So we protest it, and if we don't get a satisfactory answer from them, we go to the membership. If they are against it and feel as strong as we do, then we deal with the company again and try to get them to change it. Nine-tenths of the time they never do, because the company has a right to post a ruling. You know how a company is, they post rulings all the time, they come up with non-gambling rules, no-smoking rules, things that the company feels they have a right to put in.

Attention to problem-solving functions and administrative matters may entail a wide variety of specific activities. Most often mentioned by the officers were activities such as listening to members explain their grievances, discussing grievances with members personally and in grievance committees, preparing reports on grievances, and negotiating with management concerning grievances. Several officers reported it not uncommon to be called on the phone late at night to listen to the report of a problem or grievance. Many officers felt that one of their most difficult jobs was to convince members that apparent grievances did not constitute violations of the contract and therefore should not be processed. The president of D spoke of using "psychology" in such cases:

First of all, you have to know your personality. To some you can go up and say, "Look, damn it, you haven't got a grievance. How come you haven't got the sense to see it?" It will go over with that particular type. You go to another one, and say, "Could you point out to me, I'm pretty dumb. Could you point out to me where this grievance is? In order to write it up, I want to word it. Could you help me on it?" Now, that's another type. In order to do that you have to have experience with people and know how to analyze them. That's what I do. And I found out, it's pretty effective.

Administrative activities mentioned widely by the officers were preparing reports, doing audits, handling correspondence, keeping records of various types, and attending and chairing meetings. Just attending various types of committee meetings apparently accounted for a sizeable amount of time spent on union affairs by certain officers.

Additional evidence of the extent to which grievance-handling, routine administration, and daily problem-solving dominate the activities of our local union officers is provided by answers to the question which asked the officers to judge which one of their union activities was most important. Thirteen of the officers indicated that handling grievances was their one most important activity; thirteen indicated that routine administration (such as audits, accounting, and preparation of records) was most important; and five mentioned attending meetings. No other activity was mentioned by more than three officers.

Again considering the presidents separately, it is interesting to note that whereas four of the five presidents conformed to the tendency of the total group in judging grievance-handling (they said it took the bulk of their time) only one, the president of C, felt that it was his most *important* duty. He expressed his feelings as follows:

Well, our union president is chairman of the grievance committee. . . . I actually believe being chairman of the grievance committee is as important as anything, because we have personal contact with the people, and we're dealing with each situation as a person. That's the most important thing, chairman of the grievance committee.

Two presidents, those from D and E, indicated that keeping other officers' and stewards' performances up to par was the most important; the president of B felt that presiding at meetings was most important; and the president of A could not make a judgment.

Thus, in general, the behavior of the presidents in office was not consistent with their convictions as to the relative importance of different activities. For example, the presidents of D and E (who felt that their most important activity was to keep the whole organization running smoothly by keeping tabs on their officers) reported spending considerably more time on other matters: one, on grievances; and the other, on meetings. It would seem more logical for officers to devote the bulk of their time to activities considered most important. The only president whose judgment concerning the relative importance of activities matched the activities he engaged in was the president of C, who felt grievances were his most important duty: he also reported spending most of his time on grievances. Understandable reasons for the apparent discrepancy between attitude and action among the local union officers will be discussed in a subsequent section.

TABLE 12

PERFORMED ACTIVITY WHICH OFFICERS
CONSIDER MOST IMPORTANT

Type of Activity Mentioned	Number of Officers (Total N-41)
Dealing with grievances	13
Preparation and presentation of records	6
Audits	4
Attending the local's meetings	3
Handling and accounting for money	3
Keeping other officers' performances up to par	3
Attending executive board meetings	2
Trying to increase welfare of members	2
Five additional miscellaneous activities reported	5

Further corroboration of the importance of grievance-handling in the activities of the local union officers came from their responses to the question concerning the difference between a busy week and a slack week. Of thirty-seven officers responding, thirteen, including four of the five presidents, indicated that the number of grievances pending was the big difference; nine officers mentioned meetings, conventions, and conferences. Only one other difference, contract negotiations, was mentioned as many as five times. Commenting on the difference between an average and a busy week, one of the officers had this to say:

The difference is . . . if everything is running smoothly and nobody has any complaints or anything, I don't have much work to do. But if there is a lot of grievances, or people think that they have grievances and the stewards cannot satisfy them, then they have me called over to their department or they call me at home.

TABLE 13

Officers' Explanations of the Difference between
Busy and Slack Weeks on Union Activities

Explanation Offered	Number of Officers (Total N-37)*
Number of grievances to handle	13
Occurrence of meetings, conventions, and conferences	9
Negotiation of the contract	5
Occurrence of layoffs	4
Occurrence of trouble between company and members	3
Preparation and presentation of records	2
Talking to members to solve problems	1

* Four officers of the total sample of 41 did not respond to the question.

The responses to this question serve to emphasize the *critical* nature of the influence of grievances and organizational routines, as compared to other problems and activities, in determining the amount of time the officers spend on union affairs, and in the pattern of the officers' approach to their duties.

Members' reports of the activities of their officers furnish even additional evidence concerning the dominant role of grievance-handling in the practice of union office. When asked to guess what type of union business takes the greatest amount of their top local union officers' time, the members checked "negotiating grievances with management" and "listening to local union members' grievances" more often than they checked any other activities listed.

A basic, if somewhat general, image of the behavior of local union officers emerges from the findings discussed above. The energies of the officers seem fundamentally taken up with conduct of the formal routines, rituals, and functions necessary to maintain the structure of the local union organization and with attention to specific problems as they arise, primarily grievances. The officers' approach to leadership as revealed by their behavior seems to be to keep the organization together and functioning while attending to the immediate, daily, job-centered concerns of the individual members. The tendency is apparently one of reaction to specific, immediate problems, rather than any active attempt to control or influence the course of events. As a group, the local union officers of the present sample function primarily as troubleshooters whose major purpose is to keep things running smoothly within their own organizations and with management. In this respect, the present findings are not startling; neither are they entirely new. Students of labor have often referred to the "firefighting" function of local union officers, meaning essentially that officers are on call to alleviate dangerous problems as they arise. The extent to which the officers of the present sample seemed almost exclusively engaged in these problems and routine administrative functions is important and perhaps somewhat more surprising.

Officers' Concepts of Union Office

THUS FAR our discussion has centered about the behavior of the local union officers in office. It is possible that what they actually do in office is not consistent with what they think they should do: the question is whether the officers' conduct of office is consistent with their conceptualization of the responsibilities of office. We touched upon this issue in our analysis of the presidents' judgments concerning the importance of grievances as compared to their actual expenditure of time on grievances.

To assess the officers' concepts of their offices, the entire sample was asked to list what they considered to be the most important responsibilities of their offices. The responses of the total group indicated a high degree of consistency of attitude with practice. Seventeen reported maintaining records and making reports; sixteen mentioned dealing with grievances; eight indicated dealing with problems as they arose; and six listed negotiating the contract. No other one responsibility was mentioned by more than four officers. Not only did the officer group spend most of their time on administrative matters and specific problems of individual members, they also apparently felt these were their prime tasks.

TABLE 14

RESPONSIBILITIES OF UNION OFFICE
OFFICERS CONSIDER MOST IMPORTANT

Type of Responsibility Reported	Number of Officers (N-41)*
Maintaining records and making reports..........	17
Dealing with grievances....................................	16
Dealing with problems as they arise................	8
Negotiating the contract....................................	6
Planning and working for group welfare..........	4
Running the union..	3
Attending the local's meetings...........................	3
Seeing that meetings are orderly.......................	3
Twelve additional miscellaneous responsibilities reported	17

* The number of officers totals more than 41, since more than one responsibility could be reported.

It may be significant that dealing with day-to-day problems was mentioned as most important almost three times as frequently as contract negotiations. If it is an accurate indication of the relative importance local union officers assign to the two responsibilities, this finding would seem to lend support to those who argue that the present trend to longer contracts and industry-wide bargaining and pattern settlements in contract negotiations has tended to undermine the importance of bargaining at the local level. At the least, the finding suggests that goal-setting and emphasizing of goals related to contract negotiations are not important issues of routine concern to local unions in industries such as those represented in the present study. Although it would be unreasonable to expect officers and members to be concerned over contract negotiations on a day-to-day basis during the life of a contract, it is surprising that the importance of negotiations was not judged to be greater.

If the bargaining function of local unions has declined in importance, such a change in orientation would tend to modify the practice of leadership at the local level. Exerting influence in matters concerning daily grievance-type problems might demand a different approach and set of skills than exerting influence in matters relating to contract negotiations. The result would be a subtle restructuring of the tasks of leadership. An officer from B, a local subject to the influence of pattern settlements, put it this way:

The members are interested in working conditions. They will holler about as quick about the working conditions as anything else—say, fumes or something like that. If they think there are a little too many fumes, they will put a grievance in to stop that. As for the contract, you see we sign one for four years, then the money kind of drops out of the picture, and then working conditions are most important.

Once again comparing the responses of the five local union presidents to those of the total group of officers, the presidents tend toward only a slightly broader conceptualization of responsibility. Of ten most important responsibilities mentioned by the five presidents, planning and working for group welfare was mentioned three times; dealing with grievances was mentioned twice; and maintaining established rules and regulations, clarifying prescribed procedures, seeing that meetings are orderly, seeing that other officers assume responsibilities, and representing members were mentioned once each. Thus, even at the level of president, where the broadest and most abstract conceptualization of responsibilities would seem both proper and advantageous, fully one-half of the responsibilities mentioned are highly specific and aimed at grievances and administrative routines.

The findings suggest that the leadership practices of the local union officers might lack considerably if measured against criteria of high flexibility or creativity of approach. Admittedly, it is possible for an officer to be ingenious or creative in the handling of a grievance, but reliance on precedents and routinization of procedure in most grievance cases makes it unlikely. The issue of the creativity of the officers' approach to leadership will be explored in greater detail in the following formal evaluation of the behavior of the sample of officers.

Officers' Perceptions of Local Union Goals

THE FOLLOWING EVALUATION is based on comparisons of the behavior of the officers of the sample with the three formal behavioral criteria of local union leadership outlined in Chapter I. These criteria are: (1) accurate reflection of goals which union members perceive for their organization; (2) identification of the important problems preventing achievement of local union goals; and (3) performance of acts of influence aimed at solving problems preventing achievement of local union goals.

The first step in evaluating the leadership practices of the local union officers is to ascertain the goals which they seek for their organizations. More precisely, the problem is to gauge the extent to which the goals that the officers perceive accurately reflect the goals which members feel their unions should pursue.

Analysis of the officers' responses to questions concerning the goals of their locals reveals that a few basic goals stand out in their awareness. Of the forty-one officers interviewed, thirty-one stated that their locals were seeking better working conditions; twenty-five mentioned higher wages; nineteen indicated their locals were after better insurance, retirement, and supplemental unemployment benefits; and fourteen indicated that a goal of their local was to insure that management is "fair." Only one other goal was mentioned by more than five of the forty-one officers, the rather general goal of "improving the welfare of the members," mentioned by six. Other goals suggested by a few included improving job security, referred to five times, and getting a better vacation plan and maintaining good relations with the company, each mentioned four times. Additional goals were stated by only one or two officers. Among the latter were goals such as getting a shorter work week, getting members interested in the union, helping members who are laid off, improving the welfare of the community, and organizing more workers.

TABLE 15

GOALS OFFICERS PERCEIVE FOR THEIR LOCAL UNIONS

Goal Mentioned	Number of Officers (Total N-41)*
Better working conditions	31
Higher wages	25
Better insurance, retirement, and unemployment benefits	19
Increased protection from management (management "fairness")	14
Improve the welfare of the members	6
Greater job security	5
Maintenance of good relations with the company	4
Better vacation plan	4
To do what members want	4
Fifteen additional miscellaneous goals	20

* The number of officers totals more than 41, since more than one goal could be mentioned.

A fundamental characteristic of these findings is their reflection of a strong unanimity of opinion among the officers that their locals are striving for a narrow range of goals related to their members' welfare on the job. Furthermore, the tenor of the officers' remarks leads us to suspect that these goals are perceived, for the most part, as having relevance *only* for the officers' own local union members, not for all workers, nor even for all workers in the industry. The officers agree that their organizations are concerned primarily with local and immediate, economic, job-centered issues. The preponderant majority do not see their organizations as instruments of basic social change or as influential forces to be used for the promotion of even a limited form of generalized social justice or welfare. Only in the circumscribed sense that the locals are perceived as vehicles for the promotion of the welfare of their own members in their own place of work can these goals be interpreted as advocacy of change in social or economic conditions. Perception of basically limited goals would indicate that the local union officers do not perceive broad ideological purposes for their organizations. Thus, the unionism of the officers, just as that of the members, does not constitute "movement" unionism in the sense in which the word is normally used.

The officers may have believed, and failed to verbalize, that the sum total of local unions working for themselves amounts to a type of mass upward movement. A few, in fact, mentioned that unions are for the "working class," and most seemed in favor of political action. Even in these cases, however, the almost exclusive reference seemed to be to improve the feasibility of achieving purely local gains. At the least, it seems safe to say that although local union officers might endorse broad movement-type aims if asked specifically about them, ideological purposes are not sufficiently in the forefront of their thinking to cause them to be mentioned voluntarily as important. Considering that officers are widely exposed to international union literature which stresses broader purposes, it would be indeed surprising if such purposes were not accepted to a degree. Preoccupation with local aims may indicate, not that officers reject broader purposes, but that being a part of a local situation and having to answer to members whose prime concerns are local, officers emphasize purely local goals.

Only minor differences of emphasis in perception of goals seemed to exist among officers from different locals. Ranking goals in importance according to the number of times each was mentioned by the officers of the various locals, higher wages ranked first in C, second in B, D, and E, and third in A. Better working conditions ranked first in A, B, and E, and second in C. The chief variation between locals was centered in A, with eight of nine officers mentioning better insurance, retirement, and supplemental unemployment benefits as a goal (placing it in the top rank of importance along with better working conditions), and in D, with six out of nine officers mentioning "making sure management is fair" (placing it in first rank of importance according to frequency of mention).

The goals perceived by the five local union presidents, although somewhat more broadly conceived, were still quite consistent with the goals perceived by the total group of officers. The extent to which the perceptions of the presidents were typical of the group was reflected in the statement of the president of B, who explained that his members "buy a service with their dues," meaning essentially that he felt the union existed to protect the members and help them with their personal problems. Although this "insurance-on-the-job" philosophy of unionism may not represent perfectly the attitudes of the other four presidents, it does embody their general orientation to union aims.

Further analysis of officer perceptions of local union goals indicates that as a group, the officers made no distinction between goals which they perceived that the local was pursuing and goals which they felt the local should pursue. Their predominant orientation reflected an "of course these are our goals" attitude. In taking the goals of their organizations for granted, it was as if the officers seemed to perceive the goals of their union, intuitively and without question, as objectives embedded in the organization, rather than as aspects of the organization which could be abstracted and analyzed. Many had difficulty stating the goals of their locals, although this may have been only a problem of ineffective verbalizing. Most seemed not to have thought analytically or precisely about the specific purposes of their unions, but rather to have accepted traditional goals and statements of union purpose as given. In this respect, responses of the officers seemed more an expression of the rhetoric of union organizations than of the officers' own reflection. Even the positive value which they so obviously placed on unionism seemed as much a matter of feeling as of well-articulated reason.

When asked if the aims of their locals had ever been different in the past, of thirty-five officers responding, twenty-seven replied negatively, seven affirmatively, and one did not know. Even in the case of the seven affirmative replies, further questioning indicated that in their views the changes in goals had been minimal, having to do with changes in emphasis concerning concessions being sought from management. Immediate, local, job-centered goals thus seemed timeless and inherently characteristic of union organizations to the local officers of this sample.

Comparing the goals which the officers perceive to those which members desire, it will be recalled from the previous discussion of members' characteristics that goals which members support most strongly are related to immediate, job-centered benefits such as higher wages, better working conditions, better fringe benefits, and more security. There is no basic difference in orientation between the goals which members desire and those which officers reflect.

Admittedly, when given a chance to do so, some officers endorsed a broader range of goals, as did significant percentages of members. Questionnaire responses revealed that 45 to 50 per cent of members responding affirmed goals such as more organizing of unorganized plants, more support for aims of the international, and a better life for all people in the community. Even though a substantial percentage of members affirmed them, these broader goals still ranked low relative to other goals. More than 70 per cent of all members responding endorsed goals such as better working conditions, more fringe benefits, and more job security. Moreover, as mentioned previously, interviews with the members indicated that affirmative responses to the broader goals listed on our questionnaire may have been an indication of a response to a suggestion, in the form of a goal to be checked, than an expression of a salient conviction. Broader goals were rarely mentioned by members who were interviewed and given no hints as to goals which might be appropriate to mention. The type of goal which dominates the thinking of union members is the same as that their officers reflect.

Although officers and members of our samples seemed in basic agreement concerning union goals, there was a particularly interesting and perhaps significant difference between them. Higher wages ranked second in relative importance as a perceived goal among the officers, as revealed by the number of times officers mentioned it; higher wages ranked only ninth in relative importance as a goal which members thought should be sought. This does not mean that higher wages did not receive substantial support from the members: a solid 60 per cent of members endorsed higher wages as a goal. The important point is that other goals such as working conditions, fringe benefits, and job security received greater support, as did, somewhat surprisingly, still others such as greater unity in the local and more members educated about union affairs.

Further evidence of the members' attitude toward higher wages comes from a comparison of what they thought the goals of their locals should be, as compared to what they believed they were. Whereas 67 per cent of the membership sample perceived their locals *were* seeking higher wages, only 60 per cent felt they *should* be seeking higher wages. In the case of *no* other of the seventeen goals listed in the questionnaire did this occur. To put it another way, higher wages ranked second among goals perceived as being sought, as revealed by the percentage of members mentioning it; it ranked no better than ninth among goals which members said should be sought. In addition, when members were asked to indicate what they felt was the one most important goal of their union, higher wages could do no better than tie for fifth place with greater unity in the local, according to the number of mentions received.

A number of members observed that they felt there had to be a stopping place for wages sometime, or that higher wages hurt the company, or that unions were asking for too much. They did not indicate that higher wages were not needed as much as they seemed to fear some unknown consequence of higher wages. For these members, perhaps more conservative in nature, publicity concerning wage-price spirals and competitive disadvantages resulting from labor costs has stimulated a questioning of union wage policies. At any rate, more union members disagree with their officers over goals relating to wages than over any other goals.

Our findings, moreover, indicate that the officers were unaware of their members' attitudes toward wages. When asked what aims they thought their members wanted the local to accomplish, the officers' most frequent reply was higher wages. Interview responses of the officers to other questions indicated that their predominant perception was that members were interested mainly in money, particularly in the form of higher wages. The evidence does not support this perception. Certain psychologists have for some time been critical of managers for their apparent tendency to oversimplify human nature by assuming that any meaningful behavior of workers could only be prompted by economic motivation. The perceptions of the local union officers of this sample indicate that union officials may be no less susceptible to the concept of the "economic man."

Analysis of differences among the locals of the sample in the extent of member-officer agreement on goals reveals no important departures from the pattern discussed above except in local C, where members made wages much more important than in the other locals, thus tending more nearly to fit their officers' perceptions. Certain characteristics of C may help to explain this tendency. Local C was one of the more stable locals and had good relations with its management, which apparently enjoyed a favorable business climate. Working conditions were good and members seemed comfortable economically. Also, the local had accepted recently a pension plan in lieu of a larger wage increase. A percentage of the membership apparently had been opposed to the settlement, but the officers had been successful in overriding their objections. In such a case, the company was perceived as able to pay, satisfactions from adequate wages were known and appreciated, and wages had recently been a disputed topic: it might have been expected that wages would be more of a preoccupation.

In summary, our evaluation is that the officers of the sample performed adequately in Leadership Component I—reasonably accurate reflection of the goals members desire for their organization. There was an essential identity of orientation between officers and members concerning the basic purpose of the local union; that purpose was to attain immediate, job-centered, member-centered benefits. Within the general unanimity, there was a slight tendency for officers to reflect incorrectly the order of preference of the specific wants of the members.

Identification of Barriers to Goal Achievement

THE SECOND STEP in evaluating the leadership practices of the local officers is to assess their perception of obstacles believed to stand in the way of achievement of local union goals.

Two types of questions were used to collect information concerning this matter. The first required each officer to state the problems he considered to be the greatest obstacles to the achievement of the goals of his local. The second type included two separate, more indirect (but related) questions. One of the latter questions asked what conditions the officer would have changed, both within and outside his local, if he had the power to do so, in order to benefit his local the most. The other question asked what the officers felt their locals needed to do a better job on, in order to be more successful. These two indirect questions were intended as a check on the more straightforward question concerning local union problems, and as a device to explore concrete or specific factors officers considered crucial for success or failure.

Responses of the officers indicated that two major problems dominated their thinking. These two problems were the only ones on which any substantial unanimity of opinion was evident; they stand out strikingly for that reason. The problems were an inactive membership, which was mentioned by twenty-three officers, and a hard company to deal with, mentioned by eighteen. The next most commonly mentioned problems were a membership divided in what it wants, mentioned seven times, and members wanting too much, noted six times. Significantly, both of these latter problems, although not concerned specifically with membership inactivity, also identify the local membership itself as the greatest obstacle to the achievement of local union goals. No other specific obstacle to union goal achievement was mentioned by more than five officers.

In response to the question concerning which internal condition should be changed in order to benefit their locals most, twenty-three of thirty-three officers responding listed getting members to attend meetings or getting members to take an interest in union affairs. No other internal condition was mentioned more than two times. Responses to the questions concerning which outside condition should be changed in order to benefit their locals most revealed less unanimity but still generally substantiated the officers' stated perception of problems. The two critical outside conditions most commonly identified as needing change were management, mentioned by fifteen officers, and government or laws, noted thirteen times.

TABLE 16

PROBLEMS WHICH OFFICERS PERCEIVE AS THE GREATEST
OBSTACLES TO ACHIEVEMENT OF LOCAL UNION GOALS

Problems Reported	Number of Officers (Total N-41)*
An inactive membership....................................	23
A hard company to deal with..........................	18
A membership divided in what it wants..........	7
A membership that wants too much..................	6
Wildcat strikes †	5
Bad working conditions.....................................	5
Company doesn't make enough profits..............	5
Racial segregation by the company..................	4
Inadequate local union officers..........................	4
Ten additional miscellaneous problems reported	21

* The number of officers totals more than 41, since more than one problem could be reported.
† All respondents from one local.

Further evidence of the extent to which the officers perceived their own membership to be a problem is furnished by their response to the question which asked what their locals needed to do a better job on. Out of thirty-nine responses, nineteen fell into a category of getting members to attend meetings and participate actively in their organizations; nine involved getting members to understand their contract better. No other issue was noted more than two times.

TABLE 17

IMPROVEMENTS OFFICERS FEEL THEIR LOCALS NEED
TO ACCOMPLISH TO BECOME MORE EFFECTIVE

Improvements Indicated	Number of Officers (Total N-39)*
Get more members to participate and/or attend meetings	19
More effectively educate and inform members concerning their union and their contract	9
Improve relations with management	2
Improve grievance handling	2
Increase officers' efforts on members' behalf	2
Concentrate more on job-oriented unionism	1
Increase the size of the membership	1
No improvements necessary	3

* Two officers of the total sample of 41 did not respond to the questions.

The nature of the officers' own expression of the membership problem may be revealing. The president of C had this to say:

I know personally that we have strong people that believe real strongly in unionism, but as far as participation is concerned, we stand back and let the other fellow go ahead. I think it's a wrong attitude for people to take. I'd like to see them come in and take an active part, run for offices—for the main offices even—take the part of stewards, be on committees, and so forth, so that they would learn what the union stands for, same as the officers we have now. . . . It's an attitude that they'll take. Maybe they'll get to building a house or something, and they'll say, "Well, the house comes first. In the union, everything's going fine. Tell them in the union meeting I won't be there." I believe that once a month everybody can be at a meeting; I believe they should take more interest.

The president of D put it as follows:

Our biggest problem is indifference. The same thing applies to schools and churches. That is our biggest sin, indifference and selfishness. You see, with us, if we don't attend a meeting, we don't financially lose anything. But you take the opposite side of the bargaining table, when they don't back each other up or attend a meeting, they stand to lose money. They back themselves up . . . which we don't . . . unfortunately. We can't see it.

An officer from B, who felt the membership inadequately fulfilled what was expected of them, made this statement:

We wish they would come to more meetings, more of them, and see how we run the meetings and things like that. That's a place for improvement . . . if they would come to the meetings, to learn about the union and find out what is going on.

The findings clearly indicate that officers of the sample perceived local union membership and the management to be the two chief obstacles to union goal achievement. Considering the goals which the officers endorsed for their organizations, it is logical that the problems of the membership and the management should have been linked as obstacles to goal achievement. In effect, the officers believed, (as did the members) that the goals of their organizations could only be obtained through modification of management practices and policies.

This recognition is reflected in interview responses of the officers which indicated almost exclusive identification of bargaining with management as the one best method local unions could use to achieve their goals. Since bargaining with management is the way gains are won, management inevitably will be an important obstacle. The difficulty of the obstacle may vary, depending on the willingness of management to grant concessions, but its presence is assured by virtue of the nature of the relationship between local union and management.

The nature of the local union–management relationship, as influenced by the nature of union goals, accounts for the officers' perception of their own members as problems. In the minds of both officers and members, a union is an organization which depends upon collective pressure against management to achieve success. Any lack of concert in action, as would result from an inactive membership, would fail to create the maximum necessary collective pressure, and consequently would constitute an obstacle.

The five local union presidents agreed quite consistently on the obstacles perceived by the total group of officers, except that they perceived unfavorable labor legislation as a more important problem than management practices. For example, three of the five presidents mentioned an inactive membership as a chief obstacle to the achievement of local union goals; the same number mentioned unfavorable legislation. Four of the five presidents identified an inactive membership as the factor within unions most in need of change; the same number identified unfavorable legislation as the most critical external factor needing change. When asked what their locals needed to do a better job on, four of the five presidents indicated that activating the membership was their prime need.

Although the presidents were concerned chiefly with their own membership, their tendency to see unfavorable legislation as more of a problem than management practices indicated that, compared to other officers, the presidents apparently possessed a more sophisticated point of view concerning obstacles. It would seem that the presidents reflect the opinion that legislation is a more fundamental problem than management because a favorable legislative climate can facilitate a union's ability to be successful in dealings with management.

In contrast to the minimal variation in perception of union goals among officers from different locals, there were important differences among locals in officer perceptions of problems preventing achievement of goals. Local A was an exception in that officers from A generally did not perceive an inactive membership to be an obstacle, (only two of nine officers from A stated they did). In each of the other locals, from half to all of the officers interviewed mentioned their membership as an obstacle. Local D was unusual in that five of its nine officers perceived two problems which were not mentioned by officers of the other four locals: members wanting too much and wildcat strikes. Three of the nine officers from D also mentioned bad or inadequate local union officers, a problem also relatively ignored by officers of the other locals. Three of six officers from C believed that not enough firms in the industry were organized. No officers from the other locals noted this factor.

The findings suggest that although certain obstacles to goal achievement tend to occur commonly in all locals, differences in obstacles faced also will occur, depending upon each local's unique situation. It is not surprising that in D, members' wanting too much, wildcat strikes, and inadequate officers were mentioned as problems: the local was beset with factionalism and recently had undergone a disruptive wildcat strike. In A, where member participation was the highest of the five locals, participation was perceived to be an obstacle by only two of nine officers. In local B, which had a contract with a company in an apparently poor competitive position in the industry, three of eight officers mentioned as a problem that their company does not have enough profits. Although as a group the locals of the sample commonly faced problems of membership inactivity and management resistance, the unique problems of each local also were important enough to have a significant bearing on successful leadership. Situational factors in union leadership can be vital and will be given special attention in the next chapter.

To evaluate the adequacy of the local union officers' perception of problems preventing achievement of local union goals, it is necessary to consider the validity of the problems. It is conceivable that the officers are deceiving themselves, that the conditions they perceive as problems either do not exist, or if they exist, do not really constitute significant obstacles to goal achievement. We can take for granted the legitimacy of the perception of management as a problem. Supporting evidence is needed to validate the perception of the problem of an inactive membership. Are local union members lax in participation? Does a lack of member participation hinder achievement of goals?

Evidence concerning the formal participation of the local union members has already been discussed. To restate these findings, approximately 60 per cent of the members reported attending only one-quarter or fewer regularly scheduled union meetings in the twelve months prior to questioning. Fully 51 per cent reported attending no regularly scheduled meetings during this period.

A more complete picture of member participation is afforded by a composite measure of different types of union activity computed for each member in the sample. Under this system, a certain number of points was assigned to various union activities in which members might engage. The scoring was as follows: two points for each regular meeting attended in the past year, one point for each special meeting attended in the past year, three points for holding any office at the time the study was conducted, one point for having been an officer in the past, one point for having served on a committee in the past, and one point for having voted in the last local union election of officers. A score of thirty or more points was possible, depending largely on the frequency of regular and special meetings. On the basis of these weights, from 60 to 76 per cent of the members of each of four of the five locals studied received participation scores of nine or less. In each of these same locals, from slightly less than, to slightly more than, one-third of the members received a score of two or less.

Although on such a basis, it is admittedly difficult to establish arbitrarily a score below which one could classify participation as inadequate, it is obvious that a significantly large percentage of union members seldom participate formally in their organizations, if at all. Even in local A, which had the highest participation of the five locals of the sample, nearly one-third of the members received participation scores of four or less. The officers' complaints of a formally inactive membership are substantially correct.

It is difficult to ascertain whether a lack of formal member participation actually constitutes an obstacle to the achievement of local union goals. A simple check on the judgment of the officers was obtained by comparing their judgment with that of union members and international representatives. Comparing the judgment of officers and members, we find excellent agreement. As mentioned in previous chapters, members identify themselves as chief obstacles to local union success. Although approximately one-quarter of the membership sample replied they did not know what problems stood in the way of their locals, those who did perceive problems listed members disinterest and a difficult management with which to deal. The judgment of the officers also matched that of international representatives interviewed in the course of study. International staff men consistently perceived members' lack of participation as an important obstacle to local union success. Several referred to apathy among union members, which they felt resulted from members having become accustomed to regarding group gains as rights independent of any responsibilities. Several mentioned a lack of interest among younger members, which they felt stemmed from a lack of historical perspective concerning employer-employee relationships.

Finally, it is the judgment of the writers that a formally inactive membership *is* an important barrier to local union success. An active membership reflects interest in the union and support for its basic purposes, promotes successful union functioning, and creates an image of vigor, strength, and collective endeavor which can be used to advantage in the bargaining relationship. Local unions are democratically structured organizations; as pointed out in the previous chapter, many of their policies and practices are predicated upon an assumption of formal membership participation. Effective union action depends upon the individual union members performing certain functions—walking a picket line, voting in union elections, or providing funds for political campaigns. Lack of formal participation hinders the operation of local union policy and procedure and also diminishes the ability of the union to exert power against management. In fact, the behavior of management apparently reflects recognition of such a relationship. As many of the local officers expressed it (in slightly variant ways), "If management sees a lack of participation, interest, or support among the members, it is just that much harder to bargain successfully with them." Conversely, according to the officers, when management knows the membership is participating and "means business," bargaining with them becomes that much easier.

The writers also believe that the extent of union members' allegiance to their organizations may be dependent upon some type of formal participation. This belief is based on the observation that maximum satisfaction in belonging to a union is obtained best through participation, and allegiance depends upon satisfaction.

In summary, considering the nature of the goals they perceived for their organizations, the local union officers identified correctly the important barriers to goal achievement. Thus, on Leadership Components I and II—perception of goals and perception of problems—the local union officers seemed to perform adequately. We turn our attention now to an analysis of the officers' performance in the crucial third and last component of leadership, the exertion of influence to solve problems preventing goal achievement.

Attempts to Remove Barriers to Goal Achievement

SINCE local union officers judged their most important problem to be an inactive membership, it would be expected that their efforts to stimulate union goal achievement would be directed toward solving the problem of membership apathy. This was precisely the case. Efforts were directed toward encouraging greater participation in union affairs through manipulation of the behavior of union members. Appropriate application of reward, punishment, or education constituted the primary effort at manipulation; typically the officers wanted to change or remove disinterest, laziness, or lack of information perceived among their members. Their prevalent attitude was, "if only we could change the personal characteristics of our members, our biggest problem would be solved." In practice, this attitude most often was transformed into attempts to stimulate greater attendance at meetings. Concern with attendance was consistent with the officers' perception of lack of member participation as a basic problem and with their concept of the meaning of participation. When asked their interpretation of membership participation, thirty-three officers mentioned "attending meetings"; this was three times as many references as was received by any other item of member behavior.

Information concerning actions officers had taken was obtained through a direct question which asked what the officers had done to meet the problems of their locals. Twenty-one officers replied they had tried to get more members to meetings. Eighteen mentioned education and informing members. Only three other different attempts at problem solution received five or more comments: educating the officers (with six), and involving the members in the organization and getting a better contract (with five each). Several other different attempts at problem solution were mentioned by only two or three officers. A large proportion of the less unanimously endorsed approaches involved attempts to modify or remove problems created by management. Hence, the majority of the specific attempts by the officers at problem solution were directed at internal problems of union organization and solidarity; also, while there was substantial agreement among officers in approach to the membership problem, there was less agreement in approach to the management problem.

TABLE 18

WAYS IN WHICH OFFICERS ATTEMPTED TO SOLVE PROBLEMS FACING THEIR LOCALS

Attempt at Problem Solution Reported	Number of Officers (Total N-41)*
Getting more members to attend meetings	21
Educating and informing members	18
Educating officers	6
Involving more members in the local	5
Getting a better contract	5
Making the grievance procedure more effective	4
Thirteen additional miscellaneous attempts reported	23

* The number of officers totals more than 41, since more than one attempted solution could be reported.

Specific examples of attempts to stimulate member participation revealed a tendency for the officers, to seek a "gimmick," or panacea, which would increase participation, usually through some application of reward or punishment. For instance, commonly mentioned programs for stimulating participation which had either been tried or were being contemplated included rewards, in the form of door-prizes or refreshments to those attending meetings, or punishment, in the form of fines or other sanctions against those not attending. Since the officers tended to equate participation with attendance at meetings, they considered any devices which would get members to attend meetings appropriate solutions to the problem of membership inactivity. Although attendance at meetings is an important type of formal participation, attendance which depends upon prodding and coercion rather than upon sincere interest and concern can only be a temporary and ineffective approach to the participation problem. When achieved by a gimmick, attendance may come to mean primarily the physical presence of members at meetings, whether or not such presence is in spirit as well as in body. For many officers, attempting to get out large numbers of members to meetings seemed a ritual which, if successful, provided the satisfaction of feeling that the members actively supported their organization, although that success may have been accomplished only with the aid of special blandishments or goads.

The writers do not deny that some progress may be made just by getting members to meetings: once there, they may become interested and come again, communications may be improved, and an appearance of strength may be built. We believe, however, that the participation problem resides fundamentally in the strength of the members' personal commitment to their organization. The means the officers advocated for stimulating attendance seem likely to fail as lasting solutions to the problem of getting members to attend meetings because they are superficial and illusory means of increasing commitment to the union.

The major difficulty with an oversimplified "carrot-and-stick" approach to the motivation and participation of local union members is that it treats the symptoms of the participation problem, rather than the real problem itself. An officer from B provides a perfect illustration of the difficulty:

Maybe a person works all week and they don't feel like getting out to the membership meeting, or their wife wants them to take her for a ride or something like that . . . and if everything is running smooth over at the plant they figure "they don't need me down there. . . . " I'd like to change that attitude but I don't know how. . . . We tried a door prize and it didn't seem to pick up the response we wanted. And we had a dollar fine; if you missed three meetings it cost you a dollar. That seemed to pick up the attendance, but the only thing wrong with that was when we got the attendance up, they voted the fine off.

A striking impression was that the officers' attempts at problem solution had a stereotyped, fixed quality about them. The attempts seemed a part of the established pattern of conduct of local union office, rather than logical and reasoned attacks on the fundamental source of the membership problem. It may have been that the difficulty was as much a failure to identify the source of the participation problem correctly as it was a failure to devise programs to solve it.

Reported attempts of the officers to solve their membership problem through education also seemed basically limited and stereotyped in conceptualization. Although educational programs could have been of great benefit, advocacy of education as a solution to membership apathy had not been critically evaluated by the local union officials of the sample. The type of education most often proposed was directed toward increasing understanding of contract and grievance procedures, increasing understanding of union history and accomplishments, and generally heightening appreciation of the philosophy and goals of trade-unionism. Accomplishing these educational aims no doubt would have been a worthwhile objective in its own right, but it is not clear that their accomplishment would have created greater membership participation.

It is not our aim to deprecate the importance of membership attendance at local union meetings or of education in the union. Both are of substantial importance in keeping a union strong and vigorous. But as effectuated, these efforts did not constitute well-considered, rational, and effective ways of removing the source of the problem of membership inactivity. Direct evidence of this is supplied by findings concerning the success of such programs. When asked which efforts at problem-solving had been most successful, there was a dearth of response from the sample of local union officers. A number reported no actions had been successful. The action most frequently mentioned as most successful was education (really indoctrination) of members, mentioned by nine officers. Getting members to attend meetings was mentioned as most successful by five officers. No other action was mentioned more than five times. More evidence is available in the data concerning the low level of membership participation, and in that so many officers identify a lack of membership participation as a continuing problem. Obviously, attempts to solve the problem of membership participation had not been very successful.

One of the key features of the officers' approach to the problem of inactive membership was the lack of variety and creativity in attempts at solution. The officers not only seemed to restrict themselves to attempts to get members to meetings and to educate them (which most often meant to tell them what the union was doing for them) but also seemed to possess a limited range of ideas as to what else might be done. In response to a question which asked whether any different ways could have been used to deal with their problems, twenty officers replied no and only fifteen yes. Moreover, among those answering yes, the dominant tendency was to suggest a slight variation on the major themes of educating members and getting them to meetings.

Further evidence of the narrow range of the officers' problem-solving behavior is furnished indirectly by the findings related to their activities in office. As noted in our previous discussion of behavior in office, grievances and organizational routines dominated the activities of the officers, the presidents included. Little or no time was reported spent in planning or executing programs which might be interpreted as attacks on the problem of membership inactivity. Even though the problem of membership inactivity may have attracted the attention of the officers, attempts to solve these problems (if made at all) seemingly fell into an off-the-cuff category, involving little expenditure of energy.

Although they differed somewhat in the specific problem solutions attempted, local union presidents conformed generally to the orientation of the total officer group. Of eleven attempts at problem solution mentioned by the five presidents, nine had to do with the internal operations and effectiveness of the local union as an organization. Mentioned more than once were educating and informing members (with three listings), and educating officers and getting more members to meetings (with two each). Only two of the eleven attempted solutions suggested by the presidents had to do with the problem of management. It might be argued that since the officers of the locals spend so much time in grievance-handling, they are in effect attempting constantly to remove obstacles posed by management. Apparently the officers themselves did not think of grievance-handling as an attempt to remove obstacles to goals.

There were differences among the locals of the sample in the particular internal problems their officers attempted to meet. For example, the officers of E unanimously reported trying to get more members to meetings, while none of the officers of A reported trying this approach, and only two from C reported it. On the other hand, three officers from A reported having attempted to solve the problems of their local through educating the officers; none of the officers of E reported this solution. Whereas only one officer from C reported attempting to educate and inform the members, nearly half or more of the officers from each of the other four locals reported this attempted solution. These findings are consistent with the diversity found among the locals in the problems which officers perceived to stand in the way of goal achievement. The findings also indicate that, though there may be agreement between officers from different locals in that they are all primarily attacking internal organizational problems, the direction that the problem-solving takes depends upon the particular internal problems isolated and the unique sources perceived.

It is not surprising that the local union officers tended to direct their problem-solving behavior at their own membership. As we have indicated previously, the problems of membership and management seemed closely related in the minds of officers in that they apparently perceived truculence on the part of management to be the result of an inactive, uninterested union membership. Although the reverse relationship might also be argued—that an uninterested membership can grow out of impotence imposed on a union by an uncooperative management—it is not likely to be accepted by union officers. Even if accepted, still the only possible constructive course of action for a local union officer would be to attempt to counteract the adverse influence of management by stimulating enthusiasm and interest among members in order to create the solidarity and aggressiveness necessary for success. The basis of union philosophy is that strength and success are based on solidarity. Local union officers would seem to behave rationally in judging the creation of interest and participation among members to be a fundamental and elementary problem: it must be the starting point for any success in goal attainment.

In summary, although the local union officers of our sample did report continuing efforts at influencing the removal of important barriers to the achievement of the goals of their locals, the evidence is that these acts were relatively unsuccessful. Assessing these findings for their contribution to our evaluation of the officers against the formal criteria of leadership set forth in Chapter I, it is evident that as a group, the officers were not performing adequately in Leadership Component III, the performance of acts of influence aimed at solving problems preventing achievement of local union goals. To the extent that they were not performing adequately here, the local union officers of the sample were not performing as successful leaders.

Evaluation and Conclusions

THE MAJOR CONCLUSION to be drawn from the foregoing evaluation is that the behavior of local union officers did not constitute successful leadership according to our definition. The essence of leadership—i.e., effectiveness in achieving solution of problems obstructing goal achievement—was lacking. The bulk of the officers' time and energies was in fact taken up with attention to organizational routines and problems of individual members. A certain amount of planning may have been done, especially by the presidents, but for the most part handling grievances, discussing "gripes," answering questions for individual members, and keeping records constituted the major responses of officers to the demands of their positions. Many of these tasks might have been done as well by "outsiders" hired specifically for that purpose. As a group, the officers could be considered no more than potential leaders because their performance did not include the indispensable ingredient of *influence,* which could have removed major obstacles to union success.

It seems a reasonable interpretation that the behavior of the local union officers may actually have tended to aggravate the basic problem of membership participation. Although grievances are important, it may be that an unduly heavy emphasis on them can magnify the importance of specific individual aims, problems, and rewards at the expense of group goals. As a result, rank-and-file local union members may be less concerned with collective endeavor toward common goals and more concerned with each individual's success in holding on to what he already has.

Active participation of members in groups and organizations will be engaged in only to the extent that membership in the group, as well as the act of participation itself, is rewarding. Continuing participation will be fostered by continuing rewards; apathy and lack of participation will stem from a lack of reward. Used in this sense, reward does not necessarily refer to financial gain but has a much broader meaning: it refers to any significant satisfaction gained from fulfillment of influential human needs or desires. The difficulty with making the protection of the grievance procedure a chief reward is that to many members who never have had occasion to file a grievance, the reward may be symbolic and remote, rather than tangible and immediate. Only a few members with problems, gripes, and grievances pending, or those in departments or occupational categories likely to be affected by solution of a problem, experience direct satisfaction. For these few, rewards are in the present and more than symbolic. Their stake in the organization is consequently high, and their participation will be sustained on a continuing basis, as long as immediate rewards accrue. On the other hand, most members, unaffected by grievances (or reluctant to file them or become involved for fear of management reprisal), will lack the stimulus of tangible, day-to-day rewards from their membership and will not be stirred to participate, because such participation seems related to little or no relevant immediate satisfaction.

In the abstract, the grievance procedure may amount to a day-to-day extension of collective bargaining through which tangible gains for members may be won; occasionally there may be a grievance which engages the attention of all members. For the most part, however, grievances are not likely to provide rewards widespread enough to excite group feeling and active engagement among large numbers of members. The paradox is that the immediate, problem-centered, individually-centered, job-related goals of the union locals can be most successfully achieved through organizational strength created by membership participation and support; yet the act of emphasizing these goals may make such support less likely.

To the extent that the primary aim of local unions is the day-to-day protection of individual union members against the possibility of negative experiences imposed by management (and only secondarily one of seeking more positive satisfactions for most members), it is to be expected that many members will be inactive and often indifferent. Protection against possible misfortune is a negative approach to human motivation and does not create enthusiasm equivalent to that which can be released by the satisfaction of attaining positive goals; nor does a negative approach stimulate widespread and continuing participation. Local unions which take the role of providing "insurance on the job" to the individual member may expect inevitably to have problems in stimulating solidarity and group feeling. In a very real sense, local unions which take this role lose the quality of groups or organizations and become instead collections of individuals.

In the previous chapter, it was pointed out that a major reason for the existence of a group or organization is that members are able to gain rewards through their affiliation with the group that they are unable to obtain as individuals.

Within the same group, different members may receive different types of reward from their membership. Homans has suggested that rewards of group membership are of two basic types, external and internal.[3] The external reward is that which accrues from achievement of group goals and may be obtained by merely belonging to the group. Rewards of this type might include financial benefits, special privileges, or prestige. Internal rewards, on the other hand, are obtained by participation in the affairs of the group. These rewards might include satisfactions stemming from interpersonal relationships, self-expression, self-esteem, or prestige. Every successful group or organization offers both external and internal rewards; not all members share equally in the two types, however. In a local union organization, it is likely that the allegiance of a minority of members is based primarily on internal rewards, while for the majority, allegiance is based only on external rewards.

Furthermore, external and internal rewards are related, and the strength and vigor of a group or organization will depend upon providing adequate amounts of both. A group which is efficient in providing internal rewards will be characterized by high membership participation, interest, and support, which will tend to add to the effectiveness of the group in its effort to achieve external reward in the form of group goals. The reverse relationship also holds: a group which is highly effective in providing the satisfaction of external rewards is more likely to create interest and participation among its members, leading in turn to efficient distribution of internal rewards. Internal and external rewards are related in yet another way in that as the level of satisfaction of one type decreases, there must be a consequent rise in the level of satisfaction of the other in order to maintain a constant level of support and participation from members.

---

[3]George Homans, *The Human Group* (New York: Harcourt, Brace, and Co. 1950).

Applying this interpretation to the specific local union situation, it would seem that since internal rewards depend upon participation, and since evidence indicates that participation is minimal, internal rewards would be at a relatively low level for the majority of members. At the same time, emphasis on the processing of grievances as a chief group goal tends to reduce the level of external rewards, as only a few members can be receiving tangible and immediate satisfaction related to the achievement of this external goal.

Still, union members do receive important satisfactions from their membership. The evidence indicates that the majority of members seem to be receiving significant external rewards, chiefly in the form of feelings of security, relatively higher wages and better working conditions, and recognition of an opportunity to participate if one so desires. It is nevertheless questionable whether the amount of external reward is sufficient to compensate for the lack of internal reward or, for that matter, whether it is sufficient to stimulate participation so as to create a situation in which internal rewards are possible.

Some economists believe that there are indications that unions have reached a point of diminishing returns in their quest for money wages: relative to past gains, future gains in the form of money wages and working conditions are likely to be less. This state of affairs seemingly is, and will continue to be, occasioned by the vigorous post–World War II economic development of foreign economies, which at present are increasingly capable of competing with American producers. American firms, long shielded from the rigors of price competition at home and in foreign markets, find themselves confronted by the need either to increase productivity or ward off money wage increases sought by unions in order to combat the advantage of low money wage labor held by foreign firms. If this is the case, the level of both external and internal rewards apparent to the union members may continue to decrease.

An implication of what we are saying is that although major problems of local unions today may be related to membership participation, the source of the problems would seem to lie more deeply in the structure and goals of local union organizations than in the nature of local union members. The crux of the local union officers' apparent failure as leaders may lie chiefly in their inability to perceive that the lack of participation among their members is because of insufficient support by internal or external rewards. Members will not participate if they receive no satisfaction from the act of participation itself or if they do not feel that such participation is relevant to their welfare or the welfare of others important to them. The officers' mistake may be a confusion of cause and effect: they tend to perceive the failure of their organizations to stem from the inadequacy of their members; the more accurate interpretation may be that the inadequacy of the members stems from the failure of the organizations. The real basis of the problem which the local unions face is, not human nature, but the nature of unions. Door-prizes and refreshments at meetings will not create meaningful and continuing support and participation because they do not constitute the kind of satisfaction which strengthens the fundamental bond between individual and group.

The structure, policy, and practices of the local unions studied have failed to change sufficiently to keep pace with a changing relationship between union members and their organizations. Effecting changes in union policy aimed at providing a more adequate set of satisfactions to members (and thus, to stimulate greater allegiance and participation) would seem to be the real task of local union leadership. Impetus to change will have to come from persons in a position to exert influence—in other words, from the officers. The failure of local union leadership is a failure to remove the problem of inadequate member participation; but it is also, and more fundamentally, a failure to influence change in the direction of establishing an organizational structure and a set of organizational goals which would stimulate more intense personal commitment to unionism on the part of union members.

Perhaps the word failure is too extreme. The local unions have not been completely successful in removing obstacles to goal achievement, but neither have they been completely unsuccessful. Few organizations effectively actualize all of their potentialities. Perhaps our judgment of the union officers should involve a recognition of what is reasonable success in leadership, considering the circumstances. By other criteria, the officers might not have been judged ineffective leaders.

Leader behavior can be conceived to involve both a *maintenance* and a *task* function.[4] Successful maintenance would entail preservation of present levels of organizational strength and morale, and perpetuation of policies and procedures which constitute the chief means of goal achievement. The maintenance function is directed toward keeping an organization functioning, while the task function is aimed at maximizing the purposes of the organization. In a union organization, the prime task is to maximize the internal and external rewards of membership. Our definition of leadership emphasizes the task function. In this function, the officers of the sample could not be judged altogether successful. As maintenance specialists they seem more successful.

Adequate maintenance of a local union, which may mean merely preserving its existence, is a legitimate aim serving an important purpose for union members. The nature of unions is such that their very existence seems enough to provide important minimum satisfactions to members. In a sense, considering the obstacles the local union officers faced, they were performing adequately as leaders, if only in a maintenance

---

[4]David Krech, Richard S. Crutchfield, and Egerton L. Ballachey, *Individual in Society* (New York: McGraw-Hill Book Co., 1962), p. 433.

role. Maintenance, without the forward thrust of maximization of the task function of an organization, cannot be considered complete leadership, however. On this point we would defend our definition of leadership and our judgment that the union officers as a group fail in the leadership function. Although maintenance is necessary (because without it no goal achievement is possible), in the long run exclusive attention to maintenance may lead to stagnation and decline of organizations. Concern with the task function of leadership, with its emphasis on adequate fulfillment of purpose and potential, tends to stimulate vigor and growth. The failure of the union officers to stimulate change can be construed legitimately as only a partial failure of leadership, but it may be a failure of considerable importance.

The findings of the present study do not suggest that the failure of leadership of which we speak is a result of any lack of sincerity, dedication, or effort on the part of local union officers. Rather, the practices of the officers are to a substantial degree a product of situations, pressures, and circumstances over which they can exert little control. An analysis of the factors which influence the behavior of the officers follows in the next chapter.

5. The Causes of Unsuccessful Leadership: Factors Which Influence the Performance of Local Union Officers

WE HAVE SUGGESTED that the failure of leadership in the sample of local unions was not a function of chance, nor of disinterest, nor lack of effort on the part of the local union officers, but a result of certain more specific pressures and influences. These pressures and influences may properly be termed the *causes* of inadequate leadership. They are associated with the characteristics of local union organizations, members, and environments, and also with certain characteristics of the officers themselves. Specific influences to be discussed in this chapter include the political structure of the local union, the attitudes and expectations of local union members, the officers' conceptions of their unions and their own functions within them, the preparation of the officers for the responsibilities they face, the policies and practices of management, the structure of local-international union relationships, and trends in labor-management relations. A case study of contrasting conditions and leadership practices in an effective, as opposed to an ineffective, local union is presented as a concrete illustration of the practical implications of these influences.

Pressures from the Membership: The Democratic Context

IT IS DIFFICULT to analyze leadership in isolation from the members of the group or organization in which leadership occurs. We have defined, discussed, and evaluated the leader behavior of the local union officers as a process in which officers influence members. In analyzing the performance of the officers, it is equally important to consider the extent to which officers are influenced by members. It is especially important to consider the influence of members over potential leaders when studying a democratically structured group such as a local union. In a democratic group or organization, officers must be cognizant of and responsive to the wishes of group members. Realization of this condition is encouraged by having officers stand for election periodically, at which time members can replace them, if dissatisfied.

The existence of a democratic political structure in the industrial type union organization is recognized widely. (The nature of this structure has been discussed in Chapter III.) The existence of a democratic structure implies that officials of locals must normally respond to the expectations of a majority of the voting members. Although some of the expectations of the members may be shaped by the officers themselves, our data indicate that the desires of local union members are far from being completely subject to the influence of officers. Differences between members and officers do exist; where they do, the behavior of officers is likely to be influenced by the differences. Where no differences exist, our findings suggest that the officers comply with the wishes of the members.

It has been pointed out that by far the most common form of formal participation by members in their local unions is the act of voting in elections. If members are dissatisfied, this act will usually result in turning incumbent officers out of office. The local union officers of the present sample recognized this fact of political life by indicating by a wide margin that they felt the opinion of their members was the one most important thing to consider when an important decision had to be made. Nineteen of the sample of officers mentioned the membership in this connection. The next most commonly mentioned factor to consider was management, listed eight times. Four officers held the membership and management factors to be equally important.

It seems clear that the tendency for local union members to evaluate the behavior of their officers is an important factor in the minds of the officers and probably exerts influence over the officers' approach to leadership. Opinions and expectations of members must therefore be weighed when attempting to account for the behavior of the officers.

TABLE 19

Factors Officers Feel Are Important to Consider When Making a Decision

Factor Reported	Number of Officers (Total N-41)
Opinion of the membership	19
Opinion of the management	8
Officers' own judgment of right or wrong	5
The membership *and* management	4
Depends on the situation	3
Opinion of other officers	1
Economic conditions	1

Pressures from the Membership: Concepts of Unionism

THE CONCEPT OF UNIONISM held by local members is one of the fundamental facts with which local union officers must come to terms. It was indicated in Chapter III that the local union members of the sample predominantly tended to view their organizations within a context of purely local and immediate concerns. Unions were perceived much as buffers standing between employers and employees: they were seen as a form of protection from the power of employers and as vehicles by which members might seek improvements in matters related to employment and the job. For the means to obtain these functional ends, local members again perceived the local unions' resources, especially bargaining between local union officers and the employer, backed up by union power in the form of a strike threat. In addition, there was an overriding tendency to desire moderate means of accomplishing aims. Although in general members apparently were convinced that the strength of their unions depended upon the ability to strike, bargaining and even compromise were deemed preferable and often sufficient means.

Attitudes toward employers seemed to constitute integral aspects of the local union members' concepts of unionism. Although some members were militantly antimanagement, as indicated in Chapter III, the majority did not seem very hostile or antagonistic toward their employers. In response to a questionnaire item concerning how they felt about their companies as places to work, 58 per cent of members surveyed rated their companies good or excellent in treatment of workers, another 32 per cent rated their companies in a medium category (neither good nor bad in treatment of workers), and only 6 per cent rated their companies as poor or very bad in treatment of workers. Moreover, substantial numbers of union members seemed to be aware of problems which their employers faced and their own dependency upon their employer's success. Although most seemed to desire improvements in the conditions of their employment, a large proportion also seemed to desire cooperative and profitable relations with the company. Some members were quite explicit in stating that they felt their unions should be careful not to make demands so excessive that the competitive position of their employer would be damaged. One member put his feelings this way:

I think our aims should be kept at a reasonable level. . . . There is a stopping place somewhere. . . . I would say that a company could possibly do better if things would stabilize and we knew and the company knew where they were at. . . . I don't think it's good if our demands grow and grow and make it harder on the company.

The same member, changing orientation slightly, commented further:

We should have a better local. I don't mean a local that would make it hard on the company. I mean a local whose men would work with the company, understand the company's problems, and the company would try to understand us. . . . There should be a better relationship between the company and the union. . . . I like to co-operate with my boss and do a good day's work, and he pays me for a good day's work whether I make it or not. . . . After all, the company pays you, and you should have some respect for the company you work for. I don't think a lot of the men understand that. They don't realize that the company has to make the money that they pay them with.

Analysis of the total interview of this member reveals another vital point: he was not antiunion. He desired a strong union which would stand up for the rights of employees. At the same time, he did not feel that a strong union should damage the company or enter into serious conflict with it.

Many officers shared similar sentiments. An officer from C observed:

I believe we owe the company the loyalty to give them a fair day's work. I believe that we ought to live up to the company rules and regulations—in other words be fair with the company the same as we are with each other. We couldn't have a union without a company. . . . Your loyalty is there too, to the individual company, because they are based in a competitive economy.

An officer from B commented on how the union could best accomplish its aims:

We can reach our goals partially through automation. Even though we are a small company, we are getting somewhat automated, and I think through automation they are turning out more production and getting it done cheaper. As a result, they are making more money, and by them making more money we have a right to get some of the things we want.

Attitudes of this sort seem consistent with conceptualizing unionism as basically a local matter; many members seemed to perceive unionism as a relatively limited relationship between an employer and employees. The success of such a relationship apparently was perceived to depend upon a healthy and co-operative employer, just as much as upon a strong and vigorous union. These attitudes are in harmony with the much discussed concept of "dual allegiance," which holds that union members feel no incompatibility in giving allegiance to both their employer and their union.[1]

Some union members actually seemed unable to conceptualize their unions in isolation from their companies. In these cases, the functions of union and company were so related in the minds of members as to suggest that company and union were both accepted, implicitly and unquestioningly, as integral and inseparable aspects of the general employment situation. The existence and role of both were simply perceived as permanent fixtures of the total reality which was the world of work. Furthermore, these members apparently did not perceive the union to depend completely upon the employer, or vice versa. The local union–employer relationship was something which was "just there," for the most part existing in the background of awareness until conflicts or problems arose to make it salient. For such members, a local union has no meaning without the employer and the job; no fundamental conflict between union and employer is deemed necessary nor, in some cases, is the possibility even perceived.

Local union members' concepts of unionism would logically be expected to shape their opinions of desirable relationships

---

[1]Theodore V. Purcell, "Dual Allegiance to Company and Union—Packing House Workers," *Personnel Psychology* VII (1954), 48-58.

between union and company. When asked whether they thought their unions had any responsibility or obligation to their companies, 73 per cent of the membership sample replied "yes." The specific obligations most prevalently checked by the members were: to be fair and square, to make suggestions about how the company can improve itself, and to decrease demands when necessary to keep the company competitive. Predominantly, the members seemed to want their unions and their employers to work together in harmony in order to maximize the strength of both, thereby maximizing the benefit to the members.

The expectations which local union members possess concerning relations between union and employer will tend to determine what they expect of their local union officers. When asked specifically what they expected of their officers, the largest percentage of the local union members indicated that they expected officers to be honest and fair with both union members *and* management. Although a large percentage also indicated that they expected officers to be tough bargainers with management, only half as many members endorsed this expectation as endorsed being honest and fair.

The meaning for the task of the local union officer would seem to be that as chief executor of the union role in the union-employer relationship, the officer can satisfy a substantial percentage of his membership only by achieving improved conditions of employment through negotiation, but *without* rancor or conflict and *without* damaging either union members or company in the process. The officer will be judged, not solely in terms of his relationship to members, but also in terms of his relationship to management. Since a large number of local union members apparently feel dependent upon both employer and union, they are likely to favor the union officer who can accomplish their aims within a climate of harmony between company and union; for an officer to do so is difficult.

These expectations seem to place the local union officer in the difficult position of having to win grievances and drive hard bargains with an employer without disturbing the status quo of relations between the employer and union members. If this analysis is correct, in effect the job of the local union officer becomes partially one of labor relations. This could explain some of the tendency prevalent among officers to spend so much time on grievances and day-to-day problems of member-employer relations, and could explain further why the union presidents in particular seemed concerned over their ability to keep both their members and the employer happy. In order to serve their members adequately, it was necessary for them to satisfy the desires of the members for protection against the uncertainties of daily relationships with the employer while simultaneously maintaining co-operative relations with the employer. Such a task is demanding, time-consuming, and subject to failure.

Unless an employer is unusually co-operative, some conflict is almost certain to ensue if a local union officer presses his members' problems and grievances vigorously. The officer will lose favor with most members, and particularly with the more militant, antimanagement members, if he does not press vigorously for concessions from the employer. On the other hand, he will lose favor with members more neutral toward management if harmony between company and union is upset. As a result, to stay in office a local union officer, especially a president, seemingly must walk a tightrope of attempting to gain new ground for members without alienating the employer. In this sense, the local union officer is a "man in the middle" between union members and employer: he must be a labor relations practitioner.

It is to be recognized that attitudes of union members toward the desirability of peaceful relations with an employer will vary with their assessment of conditions of employment and their relative satisfaction with the work situation. Differences between locals and within locals as to the desired relationship of local union officer to employer are to be expected. All local union members will not judge officers by the amount of harmony existing between company and union. There may be enough members who do, however, to create a block of opinion of sufficient size to necessitate appropriate response from officers within the democratic political structure of the local union. Within the present sample of union members, positive feelings toward employers predominated. It is reasonable to assume that in a time of relative prosperity and increasingly enlightened employee relations, positive or neutral feelings toward employers would not be unusual. Such feelings might also be widespread in a climate of apprehension concerning management's ability to furnish jobs. Where such feelings do predominate, union officers are not likely to gain favor with union members by attacking or obstructing the employer too aggressively. Rather, officers probably will have to depend upon more subtle means of dealing with employers and may even have to experiment with alternative approaches to satisfying members' desires.

Pressures from the Membership: Desired Form of Member-Officer Relationship

MEMBER CONCEPTIONS of the desired form of relationship between themselves and their officers apparently were influential in shaping the behavior of the sample of local union officers. As mentioned previously, local union members tended to rely heavily on their officers to run the union and to provide personal services when needed. Members expected officers to be interested in, and sympathetic toward, their problems on the job and to have their best interests at heart. Officers who held favor with members had to be militantly *for* the members; yet, as suggested above, it would have been dangerous for them to be obviously *against* the employer. Officers were expected to be protectors, advisors, and sounding boards for gripes, and were further expected to possess the expert knowledge necessary to solve any and all problems. Many members took the attitude that since they paid dues, they had an expert service due them; officers were expected to produce the service when members were in trouble or had concrete problems with management or the job.

An implication of these expectations and attitudes of union members is that officers who, through skill, power, or influence with an employer, can solve the personal problems of members, gain influence and stature in their organizations; officers who fail in solving problems lose stature. The extent to which officers can exert influence in their own organizations may depend significantly upon their success in influencing the employer in the solution of personnel problems involving union members. The reverse relationship would also seem to hold: the more influence an officer has within his local union, the more apt he is to be able to influence solution of problems with the employer. In this type of situation, successful leadership depends upon more than good interpersonal relations with union members, being well liked, dominant, or able to persuade members. It depends also upon having the specific skills necessary to deal successfully every day with a powerful influence external to the union organization.

Apparently the officers were aware of the tendency of their members to desire officers to attend to their personal problems. When asked what they felt members expected of them, twenty-seven of the forty-one officers replied that members expected them to deal with any issues brought to their attention. No other specific expectation of the members was mentioned by more than four officers. The president of C commented:

The members expect me to represent them, to listen to their troubles. You have to have a sympathetic ear; you have to understand a man's problem, try to explain things to him. . . . They want you to get their point across, especially in a grievance, whatever the grievance is.

The officers also made apparent that they realized well that their lives in office were dependent to a great degree upon meeting members' expectations of personal service. However, it was not clear to the authors whether top local union officers would have necessarily had to handle so many grievances and personal problems themselves, or whether more of these problems might not have been delegated to others, thereby freeing top officers to deal with larger issues.

TABLE 20

OFFICERS' PERCEPTION OF WHAT
MEMBERS EXPECT OF THEM

Expectation Mentioned	Number of Officers (Total N-41)*
To deal with issues the members bring to them	27
To treat members fairly and honestly	4
To represent and protect members' interests	4
That officers should *be* the union	4
Ten additional miscellaneous expectations mentioned	14

* The number of officers totals more than 41, since more than one expectation could be mentioned.

Members' Conception of Their Own Union Roles

ANOTHER ASPECT of the actions and expectations of the union members which influenced leadership performance of local union officers was the manner in which the members conceived and carried out their own roles in their organizations. Although most members seemed to believe they should participate in the affairs of their locals, few did. Most members abdicated any responsibility for carrying out or even helping to direct the day-to-day, routine operations necessary to sustain their union. For the most part, officers consequently carried the whole load.

The lack of formal participation by members seemed at least partially responsible for the officers' relatively heavy commitment of time and energy to the routine operations necessary to keep their organizations functioning. As part-time, unpaid officials with limited amounts of time to spend on union duties, the local officers could ill afford to have their attention thus dominated. In addition, the members' lack of participation probably made it more difficult for the officers to deal with employers effectively.

Interviews with members indicated that limited participation may have been a function partially of a limited conception of participation. Even though they felt they should participate, most members apparently meant by this that they should vote in elections or occasionally go to meetings. Serving on committees or taking a more continuous role in union affairs was not an important part of their thinking. Furthermore, a number of members expressed the attitude that since the officers were elected, basically the officers were the union and rightly had all the responsibility for seeing that union affairs ran smoothly. Anyone who sought office should expect to have to carry the total burden of responsibility if elected. Otherwise he should not seek it. Operating under such handicaps, it is perhaps not to be expected that local union officers can easily meet the criteria of successful leadership.

Lack of Member Solidarity

ONE FINAL WAY in which the actions and attitudes of the local union members apparently influenced the performance of the union officers was through the impact of differences of attitudes among the members. Conflicts and factions among members will be found in most democratic organizations; throughout this presentation we have noted repeatedly instances of disagreement and difference among the members of the locals over goals, over means, over proper attitudes toward employer, over what is expected of local union officers, and over many other matters. If of a seriously divisive nature, such conflicts, combined with the members' lack of participation, would seem to add to a tendency already noted —that the locals are collections of individuals, rather than groups in the ideal sense of the word.

In the more perfect group context (with cohesiveness, common goals, formal participation, and interaction among members), the task of leadership is made relatively simple, because members will work together freely and naturally to overcome obstacles preventing attainment of goals. Personal goals and group goals coincide in the group: members who work for their own welfare will contribute at the same time to the welfare of the group, and vice versa. Independent effort, participation, and commitment to the group and its purpose are likely to exist to a high degree. Influencing members of the more perfect group toward achievement of group goals requires little effort on the part of the leader.

On the other hand, a mere collection of individuals or subgroups will tend to pursue independent and perhaps conflicting goals. In this type of situation, the welfare of the whole group (or more properly, collection) is of secondary importance, with members working at cross-purposes or (perhaps more commonly) not working at all. The most pressing objective of a potential leader facing such a situation is to rebuild a more ideal group atmosphere, for without it no effective influence toward achievement of goals will be possible.

Summary: Member Attitudes

IF WE BRIEFLY REVIEW the influence of the local union members upon the behavior of the local union officers, several key points may be noted. Members' attitudes, expectations, and behavior do not easily yield to manipulation by officers. Officers, if for no other reason than the necessity of maintaining themselves in office, must respond to the sometimes dysfunctional attitudes and expectations of members. Through such response, officers may be led to engage in practices which do not contribute to effective leadership as we have defined it. Specifically, they are forced to attend to personal problems, perform day-to-day caretaking functions, and maintain a desired level of positive relationship between the local union and employer. All this must be accomplished while advancing the larger aims and purposes of the union and, further, must be done within a setting which could, at best, be termed a less than ideal type of group structure.

Personal Limitations of the Officers: Conceptions of Unionism and Union Leadership

HAVING DISCUSSED the influence of local union members upon the behavior of local officers, we now turn to characteristics of the officers themselves which tend to shape their approach to leadership. One of these characteristics is an apparent circumscription of the officers' concept of unionism and the process of leadership in unions. We have seen that the rank-and-file union members predominantly perceived their unions as local organizations, with local concerns, influenced primarily by local situations and conditions. Many of the officers perceived their organizations in an identical fashion; their views were that unionism was simple, uncomplicated, and unchanging. It can be argued that the characteristics the officers perceive are the virtues which have led to strength and progress in American labor, that unswerving dedication to simple, job-centered unionism has worked to the advantage of the labor movement, keeping unions close to attainable "bread and butter" issues which attract and unite workers. However true the contention is, it is not at all certain that the means to past success indicate the most fruitful way to future growth. Nor is it clear that the traditional approaches to unionism are as functional today as in even the recent past.

Within the framework of the present discussion, we will examine first the realities of the officers' conceptions. With growth in the size and complexity of society and the economy, it is increasingly difficult to isolate any local situation from the influence of broader trends and conditions. With increasing mobility of the labor force, improved transportation of goods, improved communications, the rise of automation, prospects for greater freedom of trade across national boundaries, and many other changes, various units and institutions within a society and the economy function increasingly as interdependent parts of a whole.

Although the local union officers apparently recognized the facts of social, economic, and political change, our impression is that they were unable to appreciate the potential implications of change for unions in general or for their own local situation or problems in particular. Many of the local union officers did not place their local unions in the context of society or even of a larger union movement. Although they were not asked any one question which provides direct evidence of this tendency on their part, the general tenor of their answers to many questions indicates that the tendency was present and strong. For example, the point of view of the officers concerning the goals, means of attainment, and problems of local unions, and the general belief that these have always been the same and will always be the same, seems to reveal a circumscribed and rigid concept of unionism and the forces which might influence it. Another example is that although the officers were intensely aware of the growth of automation with its attendant problems—and particularly of its threat to unions and the welfare of union members—slightly less than one-third of them felt that union members had any power to do anything about unemployment caused by automation. Apparently there was no strong hope that unions could change customary policies and practices so as to be able to do something about automation.

An additional example of the officers' difficulty in fitting their organizations into a matrix of change was the rather prevalent complaint that union members were not what they used to be, with the implication that members of past eras were more appreciative of their organizations. An officer from C commented:

Our older people . . . know what we have accomplished concerning wages, insurance, pensions, and so forth. They haven't changed. It's only the new people that come in and take everything for granted who make it hard. We officers try to educate them to the fact that this was accomplished through everybody working together as a group.

Again, although there was an evident awareness of change, the possibility that unions may have to modify their structure to accommodate a changing membership was apparently not considered seriously. On the contrary, this attitude, which seemed typical of most of the officers, implicitly assumes that union structure is adequate and members inadequate, and that members therefore will have to change to accommodate themselves to the union.

The noteworthy feature of these findings is that although the officers of the five local unions recognized that their organizations existed in a dynamic and rapidly changing world, they conscientiously and unquestioningly continued to follow traditional, long-established concepts and practices of unionism. It has, of course, not been proved that it is necessary for unions to change tried and successful procedure and policy. There are strong indications that the time may be approaching when it will be necessary to assess traditional patterns, however. The circumscription of the officers' conception of unionism would seem to limit effectively the possibility of such an assessment—accordingly limiting the possibility of change, even if desirable. It is the opinion of the writers that the officers did not lack the ability to understand political and social change and to weigh its impact upon their organizations, but rather they lacked the *opportunity* to sharpen their insights.

The officers' tendency to be tradition-bound extended to their conceptions of their own and their members' roles in union organizations. The officers' opinions as to how local union offices should be conducted apparently followed long-established custom: their dominant pattern of behavior in office was a problem-solving, caretaking approach to leadership. No other approaches seemed to be widely perceived; officers were very similar in this respect, both within and among the local unions of the sample. Leading a local union was apparently not defined in the minds of the officers as a task which demanded a broad or creative approach to responsibilities. Excluded from their definition were potential acts of leadership such as influencing members to innovate goals, creating new policy concerning internal operations of the union, attempting to build a more adequate group context through manipulation of the structure of the local union, or exploration of novel ways of drawing more members more actively into the affairs of the local. It seems obvious that if such potential leadership acts are excluded from the officers' definition of local union office, they are not likely to be practiced. If a broad approach to local union leadership is desirable, broadening the conceptual systems of local union officers is a prerequisite.

The officers' conceptions of what could and should be expected from their members showed similar circumscription. In response to a question concerning the desired role of members in union affairs, three out of every four officers indicated that their chief expectation was that members should participate through attendance at meetings. A few officers thought that the membership role might include other forms of participation, such as serving on committees, having a union attitude, and supporting the union and its officers. Basically, however, the officers tended to equate membership participation with attendance at meetings.

These findings tend to indicate that the officers accepted the members' willingness to let the officers perform the work necessary to keep the union running. Few officers seemed to conceive of the possibility of stimulating greater participation among members in the day-to-day affairs of the local. Few had explored the notion of attempting to seek out actively the opinions of more than a few members on more than an occasional basis, which may have been in part due to the officers' inability to perceive any formal method of inviting the opinion of members except through meetings and committees. Nor did there seem to be any great awareness of the potentially invigorating effect which more active, daily involvement in the affairs of the organization might have had on members. A substantial number of local union officers expressed the opinion that if members disapproved of officers' performances, there were ample ways for them to make their feeling known. Although perhaps true, this type of participation by complaint is still only occasional and probably involves only the more vocal members, who are likely to attend meetings and speak out anyway. Thus, although many officers were dissatisfied with the manner in which local union members carried out their union roles, they were unable to redefine the role in any way which might have removed the source of dissatisfaction.

There seem to be several reasons for these conceptual limitations of local union officers. All can be classified under the general heading of inadequate preparation and training for responsibilities.

We have made much of the influence of traditional attitudes and ways in shaping the officers' approaches to leadership. The influence of custom and habit may have been due in part to most of the local officers' learning their job by experience, by observation, and by advice they could pick up from former officers and international representatives. For the most part, lacking any substantial degree of formal education or broad experience in other organizations or even in other unions, the officers probably lacked the critical ability necessary to break out of the mold of custom.[2] It was the easier, safer, and in fact the only possible course to follow customary approaches to union office and to unionism in general. Only one approach was known or considered—the approach which experience taught, or which long acquaintance with the organization made evident.

The extent to which the officers of the sample relied on experience to learn their jobs is illustrated by their replies to an interview question which asked how newly elected union officers learn to recognize and deal with problems. Experience as a method of learning was mentioned by twenty-four officers. Help from old officers and from other officers was listed by fourteen and eleven officers, respectively; formal union schools was noted by eight; and union publications, by six. Half of the total of eight officers mentioning union schools came from one local, local A.

The officers' apparent lack of awareness of possible relationships between problems of local unions and changes in the

---

[2]Twenty-five of the forty-one officers reported that their union was the only organization to which they belonged. Of the sixteen who said they belonged to other organizations, the median tendency was to belong to just one additional organization.

broader social, economic, and political milieu may have been in part a result of another aspect of their educational backgrounds. Fully one-half of the officers of the sample reported having completed no more than ten years of formal schooling. Reading among the officers, other than that of union newspapers, local newspapers, and popular magazines, was not widespread. Although most of the officers seemingly were able and intelligent individuals, their limited formal education helps to explain their lack of conceptual tools necessary to handle the complexities in relationships among events in today's society. If such is the case, educational experiences reaching beyond the level of how to bargain a contract or file a grievance would seem a virtual necessity for creative leadership by local union officers.

TABLE 21

METHODS BY WHICH NEWLY ELECTED OFFICERS LEARN
TO RECOGNIZE THEIR IMPORTANT RESPONSIBILITIES

Method Mentioned	Number of Officers (Total N-41)*
Experience	24
Help from old officers	14
Help from other officers	11
Union schools	8
Records such as minutes	7
Union publications	6
International representative	4

* The number of officers totals more than 41, since more than one method could be reported.

Personal Limitations of the Officers:
Lack of Specialized Training and Skills

A SECOND LIMITATION among the officers of the sample was a lack of specialized skills and abilities indispensable for leadership in complex organizations. Among skills which the officers generally lacked were knowledge of legal issues, knowledge of the techniques of formal communications, facility in verbal expression, and understanding of economics and industrial engineering. Some members and most officers recognized the handicap that poorly trained local union officers faced in dealing with management experts. The treasurer of B expressed it as follows:

It's an everyday battle. The company has a lawyer for a personnel director. He represents them. We have our president and our committee, and of course our international man, but he's not a lawyer. They'll go in there and this lawyer, the company man, will quote stuff. You know how lawyers go at it; and then he has got them.

A number of officers felt their members were unfair in judging them on the performance of tasks for which they had no training. In response to a question concerning what members expect of officers, one of the presidents complained:

Some members don't know what our officers are asked to do. . . . They don't realize the questions officers have to handle. They don't realize that we have to go home and write a half-dozen letters, four or five or six times a month. Of course, to somebody used to writing letters that wouldn't be hard. But remember, all of our officers are from the local; and we're not businessmen— — we work with our hands. No, they don't understand the problems of officers. They believe that when they have a problem, you have to handle it personally. Not all of them but a percentage of them anyway. . . . They think you have a sneaky job, being president of a local.

The officers seemed especially hampered by inability to establish adequate means of communications in their locals. This inability resulted from the officers' lack of awareness of more effective means of communication or from their inability to apply better means to their particular situations. The question of poor communications in the locals was explored in our earlier discussion of the membership context; the conclusion was that no continuous and inclusive communications channels were functioning in the locals. Many members were without basic information concerning the affairs of their locals, and much information which did reach them was likely to have been passed through a grossly inefficient member-to-member channel. The officers themselves recognized the communications problem, particularly as it was embodied in specific troublesome characteristics of members, such as a lack of understanding of the contract or of basic rights and duties as union members. Members' lack of understanding of the contract was a particularly widespread complaint among the officers.

To be effective, communications in an organization must flow in two directions. Members must be able to communicate with officers, officers with members. The local union officers' own reports indicated that the greatest number relied on talking personally to members outside of meetings to find out what was on their minds. An officer of C explained how officers found out what members were thinking:

In our local we're a pretty close, compact group. We get around together; we socialize together a lot. We find out generally by talking to them, or maybe the stewards will come to us and explain what certain groups want.

A difficulty with this system is that there is no assurance that all members have equal opportunity to communicate; the system is too likely to lead to communication among social cliques. In an organization of several hundred members or more, it would be a formidable task for officers to socialize with even a small percentage of members on a basis which would insure adequate communications.

The next largest number of officers reported that they depended on meetings to obtain information from members. A number of officers were quite frank in admitting that they did not know what was on the minds of their members; one officer even stated that he found out from management what his members wanted. At best, the methods of communication used by the officers could only have resulted in acquisition of information from a relatively small number of members and then only occasionally, rather than continually. All members cannot be expected to have anything to communicate, but the absence of even informal systems of communications which reach all or most members renders it impossible for members to communicate, even if they so desire.

The problem posed by ineffective communications is a serious one for local union officers. In order to exert influence over other individuals, it is necessary to be able to communicate with them. Leadership, as we have defined it, depends on influence. Therefore, in order to lead, one must be able to communicate. Members cannot be expected to contribute to the attainment of union goals if they do not understand fully what those goals are; nor can they be expected to show interest in union affairs if the affairs are not made known to them. From the officers' point of view, decisions which take members' desires into account cannot be made intelligently if the desires are unknown. The data indicate that one reason the local union officers were unsuccessful in attempts to stimulate greater participation in union affairs was the absence of reliable communications with their members.

It should be reiterated that the officers' inability to establish more effective communications systems was apparently due to insufficient knowledge about, and understanding of, the communications process and its importance, rather than any lack of dedication or desire to improve conditions. Improvements in communications could have been made if the officers had understood why and how they should have been made.

Personal Limitations of the Officers: Personality and Interpersonal Relations

A THIRD AND FINAL LIMITATION among certain officers of the sample was the presence of personality traits which apparently impaired their ability to lead. Although we have no concrete data to support the contention, our impression is that, especially in the democratic political context of the local union, an officer's ability to influence members depends on a certain ability to unbend in relations with members. A local union officer must have the ability to get across to members a basic sympathy for their opinions and problems and a basic acceptance of them as persons, even though he may differ with their opinions or may have to reject the legitimacy of their problems. Members must feel that the officer is not only for them but also one of them. By temperament and manner, some officers apparently convey this impression, whereas others have more difficulty. At stake is that aspect of influence in a group which depends solely upon the feeling or tone of interpersonal relations. In at least one of the sample, local D, serious problems of relations with members faced by one high ranking officer seemed related to such factors of personality: some members apparently did not trust the officer's ability or sincerity in handling important issues which affected them. It is our impression, however, that traits of personality are relatively less important than other factors in determining the success of leadership in local unions. Problems such as the one faced by the officer just cited probably are rare, because in most instances an officer will not be elected in the first place if he does not possess the kind of personality and interpersonal manner that creates trust on the part of a majority of union members.

Employer Practices

THERE ARE SEVERAL WAYS in which the success of leadership in local unions may be subject to the influence of employers. Foremost is the ability of the employer to exert influence through control of the general tenor of labor-management relations.

We have emphasized that one of the chief tasks of the local union officers was the daily handling of job-related problems of individual members. Many problems of this type involve interpretation or administration of the union-management contract. Most will involve employer-employee relations, directly or indirectly, whether or not they actually relate to contractual matters. We have also emphasized and re-emphasized that local union members exerted pressure upon their officers to provide services in the solution of their day-to-day personal problems and judged their officers according to their ability to effect satisfactory solutions. The officers themselves perceived their major responsibility to lie in the area of dealing with problems of individual members. It is precisely unionism of such an individual, grievance-centered type which is most subject to the influence of the industrial-relations policies of an employer.

Relations between employer and employee are not necessarily settled by the signing of a contract. Although a union may bring its power to bear to win a desirable contract, it is much more difficult to force an employer to co-operate in making it work, once signed. Whether or not an employer wants to co-operate in living up to the spirit of a contract may have a profound influence upon the success of a local union officer. By deliberately following policies which impede and harass officers in their attempts to protect their members' day-to-day interests, an employer can undercut and weaken the effectiveness of the officers. One common way in which an employer may do this is to take a formal, legalistic approach to everyday employer-union relations, with the result that details get in the way of accomplishment. For example, processing of grievances may be delayed by red tape. It would be difficult to express more effectively than the president of D the problems that can be created by an employer who follows such policies. Commenting on the problems of his local, he put it this way:

Indifference on the company's part is a problem to us. The grievance procedure has to take time and I can understand arguing
over a grievance. . . . But we file a grievance, and its turn to
come up may not be for a week or two weeks. When we meet with
management on it, they will say, "We'll give you our reply." Well,
it might take them five or ten days to give an answer; and we get
the answer and we're not satisfied with it, and we want to take
it to top management. It takes time to take it to top management;
and again we get the answer and we're not satisfied with it. So we
decide on arbitration, and that will take a month or maybe two
or three months in process. In the meantime, it causes unrest among
the members! Naturally so. They feel they are not getting their
rights. That's indifference on the company's part.

In effect the actions of an employer may tend to frustrate
the immediate, simple, job-centered aims local union members
seek through their organizations. The threat to local union
officers is that the members' frustration will tend to result
in dissatisfaction with both employer *and* union officers. Officers will be held to be at least ineffectual, and favorable
judgments from members will be difficult to obtain. Many
local union officers have limited means to combat this type
of employer practice. Accordingly, in some respects local
union officers will be just as successful leaders as employers
will permit them to become.

The relative unimportance of bargaining at the local union
level helps to create situations in which an employer may hold
an advantage over local union officers. Because at this level
handling grievances is more important than contract negotiations, local officers will be judged according to their success
in this function. There may be no effective power to back
up these responsibilities, however, for in most cases, once
a contract is signed, the threat of a strike becomes remote.
By emphasizing their role in processing grievances and sub-
mitting themselves to the judgment of the members on the
basis of its success, the local union officers in effect commit
themselves to the position of having to accomplish goals with-

out the necessary means. Their success will be dependent upon whether or not they face an employer who is willing to deal with them co-operatively and in good faith.

In the case of at least two of the locals in the present study, locals D and E, it was obvious that employers were faced who were not willing to operate in such fashion. Lacking the power or skill to force them to do so, the officers faced the problems of unrest among their own members. In the most extreme case, that of D, a backlog of grievances and other unanswered complaints had spilled over into a serious wildcat strike. Moreover, in support of what we have said before, dissatisfaction with incumbent officers was higher in D than in any of the other four locals, and fewer members than in any other local felt their union was strong or very strong in ability to accomplish its aims. As was previously noted, the strike seemed to have been directed against the union as much as against the company.

There are still other ways in which an employer may influence the leadership performance of local union officers. One of these is through the somewhat indirect effect of the competitive position of the company or industry. Insecurity in union members engendered by employment by a company in trouble economically is not conducive to union strength. If union members fear for their jobs, they may be unwilling to oppose their management. Members may desire the union to do something to improve their situation but will not be willing to back up their officers or to help by doing anything themselves which might pose a threat to their own job security. Fear of management reprisal seems an especially strong deterrent in such a state of affairs.

Especially in the case of E and to a lesser degree in B, the employers involved had suffered permanent declines in demand for their products. Layoffs had occurred in both companies on a continuing and widespread basis. In both locals, union members who continued to hold jobs tended to be older and of long service with their companies. Interest in union affairs was low. Few members of B thought their union was strong. It may be that union members in such a situation see little potential for their unions. Their experience indicated that their union has not prevented layoffs in the past and probably will not be able to do so in the future. For such union members, the logical thing to do might be to seek security by doing a good job, staying out of trouble, and not incurring the displeasure of the employer. In a situation of this type, the union member may be afraid to file a grievance, even if he has one. Dissatisfaction with the union and particularly with union officers may be considerable, as may disinterest. The problems posed for success in leadership are obvious.

International-Local Union Relationships

ALTHOUGH both local union officers and members tended to view the local union as a purely autonomous organization, the relationship between a local union and its parent international union is an important factor in the success or failure of local union leadership. The nature, degree, and availability of help which the international can provide local union officers is especially important. Most officers, lacking a diversity of experiences and requisite skills, will be better equipped to stimulate achievement of the aims of their locals if they have the resources of their international union readily available to them. The help of the international may be especially valuable in handling grievances which involve technical questions, or in dealing with unusual or particularly difficult problems of employer-union relations, or even in handling internal union problems such as serious factionalism or rebellious members. In analyzing reasons for the success or failure of local union leadership, it is important to consider the extent to which the local in question is serviced by its international, which depends in practice upon how close the contact is maintained between the local union officer and the international representative assigned responsibility for the local.

A good example of contrasting patterns of local union–international union relationships existed among the locals of the present sample. These patterns were briefly described in Chapter II. Locals A and B from the same international were both serviced quite closely by a conscientious international representative who serviced only a few other locals in the same area. Leadership in one of these locals seemed strong and in the other, adequate, considering problems faced. There were no complaints from officers of these locals about the local-international relationship.

On the other hand, locals C and D, both from another international, were serviced by a representative who, although conscientious, had widespread responsibility, involving many other locals in a three-state area. In the case of these locals, only infrequent, brief contact between local union officers and the international representative could be maintained. Several officers from both C and D mentioned that more help from the international would have been desirable. This was particularly true in D, which had suffered deteriorating relations with both the employer and its own members, culminating in the previously mentioned wildcat strike. The troubles of D were judged due in considerable measure to an absence of strong leadership and a tendency for the local union president to engage in practices and exhibit attitudes aggravating to certain segments of the membership. The president himself expressed the opinion he would have welcomed more help from the international. In this case, the failure of leadership might have been lessened or even prevented by closer guidance from an international representative.

Although more satisfied with their international-local relationship, the officers of C, a local which had excellent relations with a co-operative employer, also revealed problems that inadequate help from a parent international can create. Local C had been organized some eight years earlier. The president of C stated that he, along with a few other officers, had built the local with little outside help, learning the hard way through the experience of mistakes. He commented (in part) as follows:

Well, I'll tell you, I learned the hard way. We had a hard job. The majority of us never belonged to a union. There were a few old-timers that had belonged to one like the United Mineworkers and Amalgamated Steel, or something. Nobody knew exactly what we were doing or where we were going. Once we set up and elected our officers, then these old-timers kind of instructed us and helped us along—told us what we were doing wrong.

Almost as an afterthought he added that the international representative had provided some help, especially on parliamentary procedure. Success was achieved in this case despite the lack of help, but it might not have been under less fortunate circumstances.

In contrast to the finding that help from the international tends to promote the success of local union leadership, it is sometimes argued that if guidance or control of local union affairs by an international representative is close and continuous, the role of local union officers becomes less important, thereby undercutting their influence and consequently their ability to function as leaders. Such a tendency did not exist to any important degree in the local unions of the present sample, except in the sense that trends toward centralization of contract negotiations at the international level may have relieved local union officers of bargaining responsibilities. The issue of centralization will be discussed in greater detail in the following section.

Trends in Labor Relations

THE IMPACT OF CHANGING PATTERNS of labor-management relations on local union leadership has been mentioned several times in previous pages. The most important of these patterns is probably the trend toward centralization of negotiations and collective bargaining policy-making. Contracts are increasingly being bargained and policy set at the international union-industry level; where industry-wide bargaining itself does not exist, pattern settlements may be the rule. Scholars of the labor movement, noting this tendency, have stressed particularly its effect in reducing the scope of local union responsibilities.[3] Increasingly, the bargaining function of local unions is being transferred to the international level or so modified as to render it much less important. Thus relieved of considerable amount of ability to influence the course of positive goal attainment through contract-bargaining, the local union can only assume as a primary role the kind of problem-centered, daily labor-relations function so characteristic of the five locals of the present study.

Centralization of union functions over the years would seem to have resulted in what amounts to an implicit redefinition of the role of the local union officer. Under circumstances which have lessened greatly the importance of bargaining at the local level, it would be logical to expect local union officers to devote their time primarily to grievances and caretaking functions of a routine, administrative type. These are the most important obvious functions left to them. The difficulty is that the day-to-day behavior of officers who perform such functions is related only remotely to achievement of the kind of vital, meaningful, positive goals that can build enthusiasm, dedication, and participation in an organization.

The manner in which the local union officers of the present study conceived and discharged their responsibilities may have been due, at least in part, to centralization of functions

---

[3]See George Brooks, *Sources of Vitality in the American Labor Movement* (New York State School of Industrial and Labor Relations Bulletin No. 41 [Ithaca, N. Y., 1960]).

at the international level. All the locals of the sample were subject to some degree of centralized policy-making, and B and E were in addition subject to the influence of wage patterns. For example, in local E, which was almost completely subject to pattern bargaining, local union officers were forced to assume roles into which almost impossible problems had been structured. Of all the locals of the sample, E particularly was plagued by an apathetic membership. The officers of E did not judge their union to be strong, and many members complained that the union was ineffectual in confronting the employer concerning grievances. In order to succeed in the day-to-day tasks which had to be faced, the officers needed to build an organization with day-to-day strength. They needed to stimulate greater interest, vitality, and participation among members but lacked control of the bargaining function, which might have provided means to do so.

As local unions come to have less influence over the course of collective bargaining, union members are likely to perceive the function of the local and the efforts of local union officers to have less relevance for attainment of positive and meaningful group goals. The trend toward centralization of the bargaining function in unions thus has two major implications for leadership in local unions: It helps define the major responsibilities of local union officers as grievance-handling and caretaking, and it increases the difficulty of stimulating members to greater interest in local union functions.

A Case Study of Contrasting Leadership Patterns in Two Local Unions

OF THE FIVE LOCAL UNIONS STUDIED, A and D possessed characteristics which seemed to suit them particularly well for a study of contrasts. Local A was by all odds the strongest, most adequate organization of the five locals. D, on the other hand, was one of the least adequate for many reasons, not the least of which was serious internal strife. Comparing the locals on the basis of specific characteristics indicative of organization adequacy, A had the greatest membership participation of any of the locals of the sample, with 48 per cent of its membership sample earning participation scores of 10 or more. In D, although the local was not the poorest of the sample in participation, only 31 per cent of the membership earned participation scores of 10 or more. Considering members' perceptions of organizational strength, A ranked as the best of the five local unions with 66 per cent of members sampled stating their local was either strong or very strong in ability to accomplish aims. Local D was the poorest of the locals in this respect, with only 13 per cent of its membership sample perceiving their local to be strong or very strong.

Comparing additional charteristics, A ranked first among the locals in that 82 per cent of its sample of members felt that their rights as union members were protected in their local; local D ranked lowest, with only 62 per cent of members sampled feeling their rights were protected. While only 10 per cent of the sample of members from A felt that their local union officers did not want the local to do the same things they wanted it to do, 21 per cent of those sampled from D expressed this feeling. When asked what condition should be changed to benefit the local most, only 10 per cent of the membership sample from A indicated they felt present local union officers needed to be replaced or improved; 36 per cent of the sample from D indicated that they felt this way. While 60 per cent of the sample from A felt their officers lived up excellently or very well to what was expected of them, only 49 per cent of the sample from D expressed this feeling.

All these criteria indicate that in terms of adequacy as organizations in the sample of locals studied, A was strong and D was weak. Successful leadership can perhaps best be gauged against such criteria of organizational adequacy. Our information indicated that union officers in A were exerting influence to move the local union toward achievement of its goals; in D this was not the case.

Among possible reasons for the varying success of leadership in A and D, differences in characteristics of the membership that formed the contexts for leadership in the two locals are revealing. Whereas all the members of A were men, approximately 15 per cent of the membership of D were women. Women members of D apparently were reflected in another difference: only 77 per cent of the sample from D reported that they were the chief source of income for their households, while 92 per cent from A reported this fact. Comparing the number of years members had belonged to their locals, 46 per cent of members sampled in D had belonged for less than five years, but in A only two per cent had belonged less than five years. Comparing total years as union members, 65 per cent of members from A had belonged to unions for more than ten years, while only 8 per cent of D had union experience totaling more than ten years.

In addition to these differences, the members of D possessed two unique characteristics not found in A and not likely to be found in many local unions of an industrial type. Members of D, although in the same bargaining unit and working under the same contract, worked in two separate plants located some distance from one another in the community. As a result of differences between conditions in these two plants, the problems, concerns, and attitudes of members from the two plants seemed to differ. The other unique characteristic was the presence in D of a sizeable percentage of former members of another international union—the United

Mine Workers. A rough idea of the number of members who formerly belonged to the UMW can be inferred from the 23 per cent of the sample from D that reported that their fathers had been coal miners. A complaint heard from a number of members of D was that too many other members had ideas about unionism formed in the United Mine Workers— ideas that did not apply in their present situation.

Perhaps as a result of these rather unique membership characteristics, factionalism was a problem in D. The wildcat strike had been apparently caused in part by factionalism. At the time of the study, scars of dissension and mutual distrust resulting from the strike remained, especially between the members working in the two different plants.

These differences in the homogeneity of the membership of A as compared to D would almost certainly have made the task of leading D more difficult than that of leading A. We have already pointed out that, in the absence of solidarity and cohesiveness characteristic of the more ideal group atmosphere, the problems of leadership mount, since divisions within the group make influence toward goals next to impossible. The situation in A seemed to approximate more nearly a desirable group atmosphere and was, perhaps, especially conducive to effective influence because of the members' relatively lengthy union experience.

Another major difference between A and D was that D faced an unco-operative employer who had followed a tough and uncompromising line. A large backlog of grievances had piled up and dissatisfaction with the labor-relations situation was high among members. Weakness and dissension in the local seemed both a cause and an effect of the failure of daily union-employer relations. The officers of the local were unable to force an improvement in the situation, either through lack of skill or power (or both), and the employer seemingly took the opportunity to block the aims of the local even more effectively. The wildcat strike occurred when a segment of the membership from one of the two plants in the bargaining unit took what they considered an intolerable situation into their own hands and walked off the job.

Although members of A also felt their employer was difficult to bargain with, their situation was not comparable, either because of their solidarity (with its concomitant power), or their skill in bargaining, or because their employer actually was more reasonable. Contrasting the relationships of A and D with their respective internationals suggests that the officers of A may have possessed more of the skills and techniques necessary to deal with a difficult employer. Local A maintained close and continuous contact with a conscientious international representative. Being constantly aware of actual as well as potential problems in the local, the representative provided abundant advice and technical assistance. The officers of D did not receive a remotely comparable amount of help from their overburdened international representative.

Another facet of local-international union relationships possessing relevance in understanding differences between A and D was the extent to which the internationals in question provided formal training for leadership in union schools or encouraged some kind of on-the-job training for officers. When asked how a newly elected union officer learns to recognize his important problems, seven of nine officers from D replied that learning was by experience; only three of nine officers from A mentioned experience. On the other hand, six officers from A mentioned help from old officers, and four mentioned union schools; among officers from D only three mentioned help from old officers, and only two, union schools. The influence of a strong, closely-servicing international union may be felt by local union officers in more than one way: not only are union officers likely to be started out with some type of formal instruction in the handling of their responsibilities, but they also have the opportunity to fall back upon expert guidance when faced with concrete problems which make it necessary. In this respect, the officers of A were better supplied with the tools necessary to do an adequate job of leadership than were the officers of D.

Differences between A and D in administrative structures and communications techniques would seem to have been partially a function of the differences in the training of union officers noted above. Considering the structure of administrative control, A was by far the more adequate of the two organizations. The importance of the control structure of local unions has been pointed out in another study.[4] Following the method of that study, members of the five locals of the present study were asked to judge how much the membership, the president, and certain administrative committees had to say about how things were decided in their locals. In essence, the question was: Who has the effective power to influence the course of events in the local? The basic difference between A and D was that in D, control was relatively *low* at all levels of the organization—in fact, lower than any other locals of the sample. In A, control was *high* at *all* levels—only one other local of the sample rivaled the amount of control observed in A. This means that members, president, and executive board all influenced the affairs of A to a high degree, while in D, only moderate control was reported to exist at any level. In a case such as that of D, an organization would be expected to drift somewhat under the pressure of circumstances, rather than be subject to firm direction.

Strong control evidently goes with effective leadership; this does not mean control only at the officer level. There is

---

[4]Arnold S. Tannenbaum and Robert L. Kahn, *Participation in Union Locals* (Evanston, Ill.: Row, Peterson and Co., 1958).

apparently no contradiction between effective leadership and a high degree of membership control. The exercise of substantial amounts of influence by both officers and members is probably indicative of a healthy organization with an effective democratic structure. It is noteworthy, however, that in every one of the five locals of the sample, the president and executive board were perceived to have a somewhat greater amount of control than members, even though the control of members may have been high in an absolute sense. In local D, the lack of high control at any level indicated that little responsibility was being taken for decisions which could have helped guide the local out of its difficulties. Ability to control is at least partially a matter of knowing how, a skill subject to development, under proper guidance.

Adequacy of communications is an additional aspect of organizational structure subject to improvement through the development of appropriate skill. A difference in effectiveness of communications was another important contrast between A and D. Among officers from A, the most commonly indicated source of information about what members wanted was meetings, with six out of nine officers mentioning this source; only two of nine officers from D mentioned meetings. The most commonly mentioned source of information among officers from D was talking to members outside of meetings. This contrast is logical, considering that A was high in membership attendance at meetings and D low. It also suggests that high participation and efficient communications function together. Further evidence of the difference between the communications patterns of the locals is furnished by members' reports of their sources of news about union affairs. Comparing A and D, members from D depended more on talking with stewards and talking with other union members to obtain their information; members of A depended more on attending meetings, reading the bulletin board, reading notices and reports in the mail, and talking to top local union officers. The methods relied upon in D are the more informal, word-of-mouth type, which we have suggested tend to be unreliable means of communication; those relied upon in A are the more formal, more reliable means.

Further illustration of differences in effectiveness of communications is provided by findings regarding how members find out what their international union expects of their local. In local A, 48 per cent of members sampled reported finding out at meetings, compared with 15 per cent from D. In addition, a greater percentage of members from D than from A reported finding out from other union members what the international expects. Furthermore, 26 per cent of the membership sample from D reported not knowing what the international expects, while only 8 per cent from A reported such a lack of knowledge. These findings reveal, not only poor communications in D, but the existence of a more limited relationship between D and its parent international.

A further indication of the difference in efficiency of communications between A and D also seems to reveal differences in the level of interest in union affairs between members from the two locals. Whereas 73 per cent of the membership sample from local A reported reading their union paper regularly, only 54 per cent from D reported this fact. Data obtained from the local union officers themselves provide indirect evidence of differences in the efficiency of communications in the locals. Seven of nine officers from A reported their members understood their rights under the union constitution very well or fairly well. In contrast, eight of nine officers in D reported their members understood their rights not very well or not at all. A membership uninformed concerning so basic a matter as their own rights in an organization almost surely would be uninformed on other issues as well, with obvious implications for leadership.

If we consider the facts regarding communications and control, as well as those regarding the training of officers, it is evident that A (as compared to D) possessed a more formal and adequate organizational structure with built-in methods for perpetuation. The more adequate structure provided the means by which officers could learn how to handle responsibilities and influence members; and it also tended to broaden the base of member participation, thereby increasing the possibility of meaningful membership satisfaction, which would in turn stimulate even more participation.

The above discussed differences between A and D combine with one last and somewhat more intangible influence: the personal styles and capabilities of the union officers, most particularly the two local union presidents. There was evidence that the president of D was not well liked, especially by a segment of the membership which felt he was too sympathetic to management. This segment was made up largely of former coal miners. In the opinion of the authors, the president of D seemed somewhat self-centered and tended to theorize and state high-sounding principles, rather than act. Furthermore, he seemed not to have established a warm interpersonal relationship with his members. Because of the many adverse conditions faced by D, however, it is the opinion of the authors that it would be an oversimplification to attribute the failure of the local solely to these personal shortcomings of the president. It is more likely that personal traits played a minor role in the total complex of causal factors.

In summary, it seems that in A an unusual combination of circumstances provided the right ingredients for successful leadership. The circumstances can be termed unusual in that no other local in the sample approximated the adequacy of A; it is likely that few other local unions would be as adequate, considering the built-in barriers to success which many locals face. The influence of a *combination* of circumstances needs to be emphasized: it is difficult to isolate any one factor which obviously contributed most to the success of A. For example, although A had excellent help from its international, local B, affiliated with the same international and serviced by the same international representative, was one of the less adequate locals in the sample. Expectations of members concerning unionism seemed pretty much the same in A as in the other locals. The employer faced by A was neither the least co-operative nor the most co-operative of the five employers. Examining the whole list of possible influences in this fashion does not reveal one factor which obviously stands out as an explanation for the success of A. If any particular factors could be specified, they would seem to be the homogeneity and lengthy union experience of the membership, the formal organizational structure, adequate communications, and perhaps the characteristics of key officers.

A general quality of A did stand out, however: the local seemed to be characterized by a high degree of solidarity and a tendency to approximate a more ideal type of group. There was an outstanding unanimity of opinion among the officers of the local. In no other of the five locals did the officers seem quite so sure of what their organization stood for and where it was heading. Perhaps particularly significant was the prominence of the bargaining function in the minds of the officers of A. There was agreement as to what was desired from the employer and how it was to be gotten. The surety and unanimity of the officers was backed up by the same type of impressive solidarity of opinion and, apparently, of resolve among the members. Positive, meaningful group goals seemed in the forefront in this local. These characteristics indicate that a fundamental difference between A and the other locals might have been that A was not as exclusively oriented toward day-to-day, grievance-centered unionism. The success of leadership in A thus seems to bear out previous discussion of the importance of positive goals for membership allegiance, membership interest and participation, and union strength.[5]

Conclusions

THE FOREGOING CASE STUDY demonstrates that it is difficult to isolate any one factor which is obviously the most important in influencing the success of local union leadership. Diverse factors interact in complex ways in specific local union situations, the relative importance of the factors varying with the combination of factors present. The number and complexity of influences on leadership which have been mentioned may suggest to some readers that the role of the local union officer as we have portrayed it constitutes an incidental and unimportant aspect of the total matrix of forces acting on the success of a local union, and that in essence, the success of leadership has been reduced to complete dependency upon the pressure of impersonal and largely uncontrollable conditions. It has not been our intent to create such an impression, and it is not our conviction that such a viewpoint is an accurate or useful interpretation of the leadership process. The preceding discussion of the causes of unsuccessful leadership in local unions does indicate that it is perilous to assume that successful or unsuccessful leadership depends exclusively

---

[5]A short time after the completion of the present study, local A expressed its solidarity and interest in positive goals by going on strike. It is difficult to gauge the extent to which a pre-strike climate in the local might have influenced the conditions we found. Although the existence of such a climate might help to explain our findings, it would not seem to invalidate our conclusions; the fact remains that in a climate where positive goals were foremost, the success of leadership and, consequently, union strength were maximized. What may be questioned is whether A might not have more nearly approximated the other locals under more normal circumstances. It should also be pointed out that our conclusions concerning A had already been drawn and put in present form *before* we learned of the strike.

upon the personal qualities of officers in positions of leadership.

We do not maintain that the role of the local union officer is unimportant. We have said that the task of leadership may be made easier by the right combination of circumstances, and some local union officers evidently face less difficult tasks than others. Successful leadership in this sense is, to a degree, situational. Practices which may succeed in one local union context may not succeed in another; officers who are successful in one context, may not be so in another. The person likely to succeed as a local union leader will be the one who possesses personal qualities and skills which meet the demands created by the nature of the specific local union organization and the conditions acting upon it.[6]

The local union officer himself is only one factor determining the success of local union leadership. He is, however, an indispensable and important factor, because he is the agent of successful influence: only through his behavior can other forces acting on the local union be translated into the successful or unsuccessful influence which is the essence of leadership. In this sense, the characteristics of officers may still be perceived as perhaps the most important elements to consider when attempting to improve leadership. This is especially true considering that the behavior of local union officers would be a factor which could be modified or controlled by means at the disposal of the local union itself. A well-trained, outstanding officer in a position of leadership is likely to be a positive force—a force which can balance the negative forces

---

[6]This is a position consistent with an "interactional" theory of leadership. The theory holds that leadership is not to be understood as being completely dependent on a force emanating from within a person or from within a situation, but rather that leadership is based on person and situation in interaction. The findings of this study furnish support for the interactional view. See Cecil A. Gibb, "Leadership," in Gardner Lindzey (ed.), *Handbook of Social Psychology*, Vol. II (Reading, Mass.: Addison, Wesley Publishing Co., 1954).

in a difficult situation. Such an officer may in fact tip the balance of influence toward over-all success. Rather than depreciating the importance of local union officers, the present chapter serves to emphasize that the problems officers face in promoting local union success vary in difficulty, as does the task of solving them, according to the situation of the local.

Although specific demands on leadership vary from local union to local union, general principles of leadership still seem to apply in all situations. Certain conditions and problems affecting leadership were present in all of the local unions studied. It would therefore seem possible to draw general implications from the findings; a discussion of these implications follows.

6. Problems and Alternatives Ahead: Implications of the Study

A Brief Summary of Findings

OUR PRESENTATION thus far has emphasized what we considered to be the key findings of our study of local union leadership. Perhaps the most important single conclusion which has been drawn is that, as a group, the officers of the five local unions did not practice successful leadership, as defined. The failure of the officers was seen to lie primarily in their inability to influence the solution of problems which impeded achievement of the goals of their locals. The crux of the officers' failure centered about their inability to solve one particularly difficult problem—the lack of formal participation and involvement in union affairs among rank-and-file union members.

One reason suggested for the failure of the officers was that they had no time to attend to broad-gauge problems: their energies were taken up with attention to details and specific complaints of individual members. Another, perhaps more important, reason was the officers' lack of insight into an apparently critical source of apathy among members—a weakening of the bond between the local union members and their organizations resulting from the inability of the union to provide members with adequate, varied, and continuous satisfactions related to affiliation and participation. It was proposed that although social and economic conditions, the pattern of labor relations, and the wants and desires of union members have changed, the traditional goals and organizational structures of local unions have not changed correspondingly, so as to maintain functional significance of unions in the lives of their members.

In addition, we have discussed certain characteristics of the officers themselves, the members, the local unions and their situational contexts, all of which influence either directly or indirectly both the officers' failure to perceive the source of their problem and their inability to do anything about it effectively. Among these characteristics were the officers' own lack of preparation for their responsibilities, pressures created by attitudes and practices of members, management practices, and the structure of local-international union relationships.

To the extent that the local unions, officers, and members of the present study are typical of other industrial local unions situations, certain implications and generalizations from the above findings may usefully be drawn. Although we have no evidence that our sample of locals was typical of unions in the United States and although no such claims are made, the experience of the authors suggests that local union conditions and characteristics of local union leadership which we have described are substantially representative of other industrial locals in the community and state in which this study took place. In important respects, they may well be typical of an even broader sampling of industrial locals. Certain generalizations, hypotheses, and conclusions will therefore be stated on the basis of the present findings. In particular, the present chapter will discuss leadership and member participation in local union organizations, the challenge of labor education, and prospects for the future role of the local union in American labor. Notwithstanding their somewhat tentative nature, it is to be hoped that these conclusions will furnish useful and perhaps valid insights into the nature of problems and choices faced by union organizations today.

Implications of the Findings for the Future Role of Unionism

ASSUMING that nothing occurs to change the patterns of local union operations as outlined in preceding chapters, we suggest that certain forces have important consequences for the future role of unions in America. It may be that the scope and influence of union operations will contract, and it will be increasingly difficult for unions to perform as meaningful instruments for the furtherance of democratic ideals in a capitalistic state.

Turning first to the scope of union operations, we find that American unions historically have not maintained a consistent, continuous range of operations. In certain instances, unions attempted to broaden their interests, activities, and programs to include many of the aspects of their members' social, political, and economic existence. Much of such broadgauged unionism failed to withstand the challenges of the times. A limited type of unionism characterized those organizations that have survived for long periods of time. For example, those unions comprising the American Federation of Labor prior to the thirties primarily espoused both the limited economic role of concentrating on issues affecting jobs, rather than wholesale reform of the economy, and the limited political role of encouraging members to reward the political friends of labor, rather than organizing a separate political party or coalition of organized labor and a specific party.

However, changes in labor's political configuration occurred in the thirties, partially reflected in the birth and subsequent development of the Congress of Industrial Organizations. Whatever the reason for the change, key personalities in the newly formed industrial unions became associated with the so-called liberals, the political left. The partnership produced an imposing array of prolabor and social welfare legislation. For the most part, since then it has become traditional for a number of national labor leaders to articulate the mutual interest inherent between organized labor and the liberal segments of political organizations.

Despite the political sentiments and commitments of top union leadership, most union members have tended to view their political behavior as independent of the structure of unionism. Political sympathies of most union members and national union officers apparently were parallel during much of the thirties and forties, but this may not have been so much the consequence of union leadership as of mutual recognition of the need for political experimentation and for political recognition of the unions as organizations with legitimate roles in a capitalist system. Most union members are not firmly committed liberals, as is quite obvious from the results of many state and national elections in recent years. Information obtained about union members for this study leads to the conclusion that many members have essentially "conservative" outlooks. This may be inferred reasonably from their lack of concern (in the normal course of events) with any problems other than those affecting them individually. While this type of orientation is a perversion of conservatism, as that term is used in an academic sense, it seems quite possible that the typical union member in our sample would tend to find his expectations realized more often in conservative, rather than liberal, political platforms and candidates. However, since our line of inquiry was not designed to deal specifically with this question, we can only suggest this as a hypothesis deserving of further research.

Despite the lack of memberships with firm liberal commitments, union leaders have managed to maintain a privileged relationship with liberal political leaders. Thus, the scope of American unionism, by and large, has included political-action programs and campaigns, at least at state and national levels. It is probable that this facet of unionism has imparted a flavor of liberalism to American politics and society; it is unlikely that this state of affairs will continue to exist unless national and state union leaders can, from time to time, demonstrate at least a modicum of membership support at the polls.

For the most part, in the locals we have studied most union members do not conceive political action to be an appropriate role for unions. Thus, solid support is lacking for unions' political ventures. Perhaps this has always been the case; unfortunately, there have been no longitudinal studies of members' attitudes in regard to this question. However, part of the value of the data collected for this study is that of shedding some light on why union members should be disposed toward union political inactivity.

Undoubtedly the major attraction of political action is the promise of obtaining some sort of satisfactions, either directly or indirectly. For a union to constitute an active political power, therefore, its members must see political action as means whereby their personal goals can be attained. However, one of our principal findings is that most of the members of the five locals conceive the locals' goals to begin and end with the members' relation to the employer. Probably people with this orientation see the only benefit of political action as that of protecting or increasing the legal standing of the union entity itself. But most union members do not conceive the legal standing of the union organization to be in doubt or threatened, as evidenced by the very low proportion of respondents who indicated their belief that laws constitute problems for the local. Given the limited, local union orientation of most members, accompanied by their lack of group, organization, and social-movement attitudes, the major pieces of legislation regulating unions enacted since World War II are not perceived to be serious problems. While it is true that local unions must now maintain records and file reports not previously required, these are matters of little consequence for most union members. It is even possible that the few local officers responsible for such matters welcome the imposition for the opportunity it provides them for demonstrating their utility to the organization. Most of the officers we studied are not very concerned with legislation regulating union operations. However, the officers, taken as a group, are more concerned with regulatory legislation than is the membership.[1]

Although political action is viewed as an important activity in higher echelons of union structure, it is devoid of widespread membership support. This means that unions cannot regularly and predictably deliver membership votes; it seems likely that organized labor's political influence will decline and weaken the vague alliance of which it is a part. Unless other liberalizing forces emerge, it is logical to expect legislation to become increasingly conservative.

Organized labor's effective scope of operations in politics may contract unless unions halt or reverse present trends; much the same may be said for unionism in the economy and society. At present, unions are finding it increasingly difficult to organize previously unorganized industries and occupations. They may not even be capable of maintaining their present numbers of members. Changes in the structure of the economy, as well as in methods of production, are rapidly reducing the importance of industries and occupations that have been the bulwarks of unionism in the past. In turn, the white-collar occupations are in the ascendancy. Thus far, the white-collar worker has not accepted the need for collective action through the medium of a union association. But

---

[1] Our conclusions with respect to attitudes toward political action found at the level of the local union are not much different from those offered by George Strauss, based on his study of unionists' attitudes. According to Strauss, "Political failure can be explained on a number of grounds. Union leaders are already overworked. Members press them to handle a specific grievance and time spent in this area gets a payoff in terms of immediate results; the rewards from politics are further off and more nebulous. In addition, it is very difficult to sell political action to a rank and file which has been conditioned over the years to think that the best way to handle economic problems is through direct 'job action'" (see "The Shifting Power Balance in the Plant," *Industrial Relations*, I, No. 3 [1962], 79).

it would seem to be a mistake to attribute the relative decline of unionism entirely to the increased difficulties of organizing. Many of these difficulties could be solved if they were assaulted imaginatively and vigorously.[2] A more critical difficulty is that unionism at the local level does not demand or even encourage the extension of the union concept. The evidence for this is the pronounced local, individualistic orientation of officers and members. They probably are (or would be, if the issue ever arose) unwilling to provide adequate monetary or other support for widespread organizing campaigns. This is so because they do not see unionism as a movement-wide or society-wide system. Add to this local orientation the employer's attempts to regain the initiative from unions in industrial relations, and the union's lack of strong, dedicated leadership and membership;[3] it can be seen that the forces raised against the extension or even the maintenance of the concept of unionism in American industry are formidable at the present time.

It is not clear that unions will be able to ward off the threats forthcoming from a changing environment. In addition to the specific internal and external problems already mentioned, it is probable that unions in American society in general are losing their fairly broad base of support because of the individualistic, selfish impressions left by their members. Whereas it was possible, perhaps inevitable, that those characterized by a humanitarian orientation would support workers' organizations during a period when workers were not sharing fully in America's abundance, it is less likely that people so motivated would be avid supporters of unions for

---

[2]For example, one approach for organizing white-collar workers would be the development of a corps of organizers drawn from the occupations of those to be organized. This tactic might succeed in bridging the chasm between the social standing of the traditionally blue-collar unions and the white-collar workers.

[3]See Strauss, *ibid.*, pp. 65-96. Strauss maintains that management is encouraged to adopt more aggressive policies toward unions by, among other things, a more stringent economic climate, in which costs are increasingly important.

that reason today. Unions must offer society something more than added welfare for their members when it becomes apparent that other groups have equally strong or stronger claims. Although dealing with the problems of a different era, Karl Polanyi recognized this condition:

Ultimately . . . it is the relation of a class to society as a whole which maps out its part in the drama; and its success is determined by the breadth and variety of the interests, other than its own, which it is able to serve. Indeed, no policy of a narrow class interest can safeguard even that interest well—a rule which allows of but few exceptions.[4]

While we are not maintaining that union members comprise a "class" in the sense Polanyi uses that term, the unions we have studied were found to be characterized by exceedingly narrow interests. The point we are raising here is that the social and economic utility of unions needs re-examination in the light of current social attitudes and expectations.

It is suggested that, other things equal, the scope of union operations and significance will contract. Most readily visible at present are the tendencies for unions to be concerned primarily with existing members and the members' unwillingness to subscribe to the unions' political functions. Including both the absolute and relative declines of numbers of union members with these tendencies, the implication is that the social, political, and economic influence of organized labor will decline. However, it could be argued that even if unionism's institutional importance is waning as judged from a society-wide vantage point, it is still possible for unions to remain important for safeguarding and extending democratic ideals and practice among a fairly limited group.

Does democracy exist in the five local unions we studied? Inevitably, the answer to the question depends upon one's

---

[4]*The Great Transformation* (Boston: Beacon Press, 1957), p. 157.

definition of the term. If democracy is defined as the ability of the majority to replace elected officers, then democracy exists in all five locals. It is our belief, however, that more than this is required for democracy. In addition to majority rule with respect to selection of officers, a number of other conditions must be met, including the following: members must have the right to dissent; the electorate must be offered candidates for office who reasonably reflect their points of view; there must be interaction between "articulate and knowledgeable" elected officers and their constituents;[5] additionally, there must be opportunity for controversy within the organization so long as the fundamental unity of the body of members is not seriously disrupted. We will examine these conditions in the light of our findings.

Among the locals we studied, there is no question about the ability of local union members to replace their officers, should this be desired by a majority of those voting; however, many of these members do not choose to exercise this prerogative in the normal course of events. The heavy majority of all members will exercise their right to replace officers only if they are dissatisfied with the manner in which events are progressing. In essence, the practice of voting by members amounts to registering a protest when events do not go as desired. This will take the form, at the local level, of voting against an officer or officers or voting to insure observance or discontinuance of a certain policy or program.

As for the protection of minority rights, the vast majority of the members sampled believe that there is adequate provision for safeguarding dissenting minorities. Very few members said they or anyone they knew were subject to sanctions for holding unpopular ideas about unions and their functions or related matters. To the best of our knowledge these observa-

[5]C. Wright Mills, *The Power Elite* (New York: Oxford University Press, 1959), p. 353.

tions are valid. However, this does not establish the absolute quality of minority guarantees, since we are not aware of any instances in which members in the past either individually or in groups promoted radical causes and ideas. But for the present purpose, it appears reasonable to assert that this condition, the protection of minorities, has been met.

There is little doubt that in the usual case the candidates for union office reasonably reflect their members' points of view. Unlike the politics of the American government, the candidates for office in these local unions do not have to be approved by a party prior to the electorate's approval. They present themselves as individuals, and their success or failure depends upon their ability to convince the voting members that they can satisfy the members' needs. Since there is an element of prestige and privilege in an office, to be voted out or fail to be voted into the post means loss of face and is therefore highly unwelcome. There is another reason why the candidates will usually tend to be reasonably acceptable. The candidates for office in local unions, especially in small locals, are much like the voters in terms of economic and social standing. Beyond this, we have observed that certain social-psychological factors are instrumental in keeping the candidates close to the voters. A person too far "ahead" of his constituency in intelligence or social philosophy will find it difficult to win elections, as will the person considered by much of the electorate to be inferior. The voter seems to wish to put into office a person much like himself, but a person he believes to be just a bit more able than himself. Although these tendencies satisfy a condition necessary for democracy according to our definition, they are likely to eliminate from elected office the members with the most highly developed capacities for leadership. Those candidates showing any tendency to do or advocate anything beyond what the members want at a given time are likely to find their candidacies subject to disadvantage.

Whereas the first three conditions for democracy were found to be acceptably satisfied, the latter two—articulate and knowledgeable interaction between elected officers and their constituents, and appropriate ongoing controversy—were not. By articulate and knowledgeable interaction between the officers and the voters we mean that the officers must keep the members informed as to goals and the means of achieving them that are realistic in the light of the existing environment. This is the process whereby the officers, from their superior vantage points, attempt to influence the process of goal selection and achievement by means of information, argument, and persuasion. Ultimately the basic policy decisions are rendered by the voters, but before that stage is reached the voters may, and usually will, articulate their objections to the officers' positions, insofar as these stem from the voters' sets of values, their own interests, or their misconceptions. Ideally, before the final decisions are determined and their administration is begun, the exchange of ideas between the electorate and the elected officers will result in successive changes in their respective positions—changes which will both bring them closer and closer together and result in the most appropriate decisions possible, using realism and cultural values as the criteria. In this way, the electorate establishes the basic policy and in so doing maintains control over the elected officers; at the same time it makes its decisions in an intelligent manner, using its own intellectual resources as well as the superior technical knowledge of the officers.

It must be pointed out that before this condition can be satisfied several other conditions also must be present. First, it depends upon the voter's ability to be both reasonable and intellectually capable of dealing with issues with the greatest effectiveness possible. It also depends upon the existence of some type of communications structure capable of transmitting information back and forth between voters and officers. While we believe union members are both reasonable and capable of understanding the issues with which unions must deal, we have already demonstrated that the needed communications structure does not exist. Hence, satisfaction of the condition of articulate and knowledgeable interaction is forestalled by the inability of the officers and voters to interact in the aforementioned manner. To a certain extent, the difficulty is physical in nature; it may be that greater attendance at meetings, for example, will bring more knowledgeable and articulate interaction. But it is also true that the great majority of all locals, including all those participating in this study, are not equipped to handle half of their members in meetings and discussions. It is quite possible that if local unions such as those in our study were to experience, say, a fivefold increase in attendance at meetings, in debate of issues, and the like, effective decision-making and administration would be impeded severely.

Although the absence of an appropriate communications structure makes this point somewhat less important, the officers of the locals we have studied have certain misconceptions about democracy that further contribute to the failure to satisfy the condition of knowledgeable and articulate interaction. Almost all the officers left us with the impression that their conception of democracy is "doing what the members say." That is, they would prefer to rely on the members for detailed direction of union affairs, without necessarily attempting to inform, educate, or persuade the members to adopt more realistic or appropriate positions. While this attitude is consistent with their interpretation of democracy, it is probably also an outgrowth of the officers' manifest desire to remain popular among the members. This desire leads them to avoid controversial issues that could alienate them from certain of the members. However, since most members do not play an active role in union affairs and hence do not provide detailed direction, the officers are left with a certain amount of freedom which they find frustrating.

The officers believe that the members' opinions about the conduct of local affairs ought to be obeyed, not cultivated or restricted; the members are reluctant to play active roles in local affairs; the majority of members is neither knowledgeable nor articulate about local union affairs. Thus, one condition for democracy is unfulfilled for a variety of reasons associated with the officers, the members, and the absence of a communications structure. This failure is closely associated with the failure of the final conditions being met.

Before democracy can exist in a substantive sense, there must be a reason to have democracy. Thus, we have concluded that within the union there must be ongoing controversy of such nature that it can be contained within the unity of the organization. This condition is postulated, since in its absence there would be no *need* for democracy; if the voters do not see a need for democracy, presumably they would not play democratic roles. If this condition were the case, an organization could have democratic procedures, as well as the *potential* for substantive democracy, but would not have substantive democracy.[6] We believe this is the case with the five unions studied. In the first place, there is not ongoing controversy involving significantly large organized proportions of the members. Such conflict or disagreement as does exist does not provide the basis for organized opposition since it centers on individual issues and matters. Our findings and conclusions on this score agree with those of James S. Coleman, Seymour Martin Lipset and Martin A. Trow:

. . . It should be noted that business unionism, as a set of ideas justifying the narrowest definitions of a union's role in society, also helps to legitimate one-party oligarchy, for it implies that union

---

[6]For an excellent discussion of the differences between procedural and substantive democracy, see John R. Coleman, "The Compulsive Pressures of Democracy in Unionism," *The American Journal of Sociology*, LXI, May, 1956.

leadership is simply the administration of an organization with defined undebatable goals: the maximization of the member's income and general welfare. The more narrowly an organization defines its functions as fulfilling limited and specific needs, the narrower the range there is for controversy.[7]

Without doubt, the unions we studied had specific goals and goals of such nature that they could be described as "business" unions. Since no substantial traces of ideological disagreement were detected, there is no basis for controversy of the type that is resolvable through the application of democratic procedures.

For these reasons then, we doubt that democracy, as defined in any meaningful way, exists in the five locals. While certain democratic procedures are employed, they fail to contain the essence of democratic spirit. In fact, their use may be dysfunctional for accomplishing the unions' goals since if they cannot be defended on the basis of furtherance of democratic ideals, it is obvious that they cannot be defended on the basis of efficiency. This is not to say that unions which do manage to develop and maintain substantive democracy are not both stronger and more efficient. They may be. However, democracy, as practiced in this case, seems to have little more than ceremonial utility.

Our conclusion is that to the extent that the locals we studied are representative of local unions in general, unionism cannot be viewed as a meaningful instrument for the preservation and furtherance of democratic attitudes and practices. Barring emergencies that may produce at least temporary cohesiveness, the unions' lack of grass-roots support for movement-wide or political activities precludes their effectiveness as a moderating or balancing force in American society and, hence, their ability to contribute to the existence of democracy outside the union organizations themselves. Internally, sub-

---

[7]*Union Democracy* (Garden City, N. Y.: Anchor Books, 1962), pp. 456-57.

stantive democracy does not exist. Furthermore, such demo-cratic procedures as do exist may hamper the type of union-ism desired by most members, a cost for which there is no discernable return. Given the nature of unionism apparently desired by most members we studied, a more efficient organi-zational approach would be to replace the elected officers with full-time or part-time experts in industrial-relations af-fairs. Such experts could be retained on a contract basis, with the contract having a life of, say, one year. They could be selected by a local-wide referendum and would make periodic reports to their clients.

Perhaps the character of American unionism could be changed, thus avoiding the conclusions described above. The following discussion outlines the conditions that would have to be met in order to attain one of a number of alternative directions for such union survival and growth.

Some Prerequisites for the Survival and Growth of Unionism

THERE is a real question as to whether unionism can grow unless it becomes something of a "religion" for at least a sizeable nucleus of members and officers. Some local and international officers indicate in conversations some recognition of this fact. After complaining about lethargic membership, they turn to some nostalgic comment about solidarity in a strike situation or an organizing campaign. While not using the terms, they are mourning the loss of group, organization, or movement behavior that grew out of some emergency situation. In the minds of these complaining officers, present members never had to fight for what they have and don't appreciate the function of the union.

It may be that for many, a crisis in life may cause a turn to religion—temporarily or otherwise. Similarly, a crisis situ-ation may weld a group of union dues-payers into an effective organization. But a certain pattern of behavior, however desirable it may be, that is founded on a crisis situation is not a firm foundation for continual action of the same sort.

In unionism, the problem is to a great extent one of building the cohesion occasionally found in a crisis into a continual pattern of behavior. The union officer sees this fact, but in most cases he does not see clearly the type of remedial approach needed. While there may be some general discussion of the broad goals of movement unionism, the "hard sell" will be based on what the union has done with regard to wage levels, grievance-handling, and the like. A continual crisis situation is either impossible or impractical. Strong, cohesive group behavior in non-crisis conditions probably must be built on something other than an appeal to individual self-interest. If not that, appeals to individual self-interest must be woven together with explicit recognition of the union's dependence upon mutual obligations to the union among members.

In the process of building the union's organizational structure, unionists seem to fall into the trap of trying to operate within the framework of the prevailing public mores. Probably most of the public adhere to a self-interested set of values. The union movement began in this nation as an effort to combat the unjust exercise of individualistic self-interest by those more powerful economically. While values may have to change in a dynamic society, it is suggested that in unionism the original values have changed too much. Moreover, the original values which prevailed in earlier unionism may even be more functional for the present society than those which enjoy wide acceptance. Unionists appeal almost as much to self-interest as any business association. But this is not an instance in which the advice "if you can't lick 'em, join 'em" is valid. In unions, the alternative suggested is "try again to build a movement based on a genuine effort to achieve social betterment."

Unions in the United States are at something of a crossroads. If the both relative and absolute declines in membership of the past few years are to be reversed, an important task is to build a different and better organizational image. This image must be built with the public and with the unions' own memberships. As far as the public is concerned, it is important that efforts be made to build a concept of the union movement that is more acceptable to legislators, editors, and others in positions of influence. Labor legislation that may be discouraging or damaging to the union movement and its continuation must be avoided. A union movement turned more clearly toward over-all social betterment would tend to remove the basis of much of the bitter criticism of unions today. This criticism, based largely on allegations of selfish union interest, non-democratic procedures, and generally uneconomic goals, would not stand up if certain changes could be achieved.

Of course it is also important, as has been implied at various points in this study, that the attitude of members toward their unions also be changed if the character of unionism is to change. The member's attitude, seemingly one of "what has the union done for me lately" is simply not the kind of view on which to renovate and expand a highly motivated, socially-oriented union movement. It is important for the key administrators and staff of national unions to try to build into the concepts of their local union officials an understanding of the great importance of the trade-union as a vehicle for social and economic reform. If our research is indicative of conditions throughout the country, the restricted conception of the union movement which exists widely at present is not a sound basis for building a progressive and highly efficient local union, or a national union movement.

Rather than withering, it is our view that the local union can be expanded in its functions and importance. The local union is the organization which, if properly administered and conducted, can help to build *esprit de corps.* Here, perhaps here only, group feeling can be built: in the local union the idea of group activity and approach to widespread problems (rather than an individual one) can be espoused. It is true that much of the basic bargaining in pattern-bargaining unions is being conducted "farther up the ladder" by national unions. Even where this is true, local unions must bargain on peculiarly local issues, and administer or police agreements: They also must have the power to build democratic group solidarity which is necessary as a vitalizing, directive force in the union movement. It is on this premise that the authors feel it is of great importance that much more be done to study local unions. Despite the concentration of economic power in the hands of large companies and large unions, the democratic potential of the union movement (or, for that matter, of the nation) cannot be concentrated: by its very definition, it must be widespread and widely practiced. But also by definition, if leadership is to be practiced in a democracy, those who are selected for officer positions must be willing and able to see the problems which their membership faces and to attempt to influence and guide the membership toward policies and programs designed to attack problems effectively. Here is where the local union remains one of the key groups in the union movement.

Leadership and Member Participation in Local Union Organizations

IN OUR ASSESSMENT of leadership in the five local unions of this study, we have made much of those findings which suggest that the local union officers did not succeed as leaders because they failed to stimulate union members to participate actively in union affairs. Such failure is explainable, but perhaps not inevitable. Although initiating change is always difficult, certain possibilities for constructive action may exist.

Constructive action depends upon a broadened understanding of the nature of the relationship between union members and union organization. Perhaps the best chance to increase such understanding lies in an approach which utilizes certain principles of the social psychology of groups and organizations. Recent years have seen significant progress in the development of theories relating to the psychology of group structure and function. Few serious attempts have been made to apply this knowledge to union organizations, however. In contrast, the fields of industrial psychology and industrial and personnel management have tended to rely on social-psychological analysis to an increasingly heavy degree. Lack of application of the knowledge of group structure to unions seems surprising, considering that among organizations in today's complex society, the local union is an especially natural and spontaneous type of human grouping (i.e., its existence is not assured by the power of external authority, as are military, government, and industrial organizations). Local unions must rather depend more heavily upon the sustaining forces of their own internal strengths. Hence, unions would seem particularly well suited for analysis in terms of the psychology of groups and organizations. The discussion following will attempt to place the problems of local union officers in a social-psychological perspective.

We have stated elsewhere that the most logical explanation for the existence of any group is that members can achieve satisfactions in concert that they cannot achieve as individuals. That local unions serve such a function is hardly to be questioned—if they did not they could not exist even in their functionally attenuated form. One may argue that a majority of union members are coerced into belonging to unions against their will. Our findings, as well as an overwhelming consensus of other studies of union members, indicate this is not the case. A majority of union members are convinced that a measure of their immediate personal welfare depends upon the existence of their union organizations.

Serving a collective function does not, however, insure union strength. The strength of an organization depends heavily upon the relative importance of its collective function to members: the more important the function, the greater the allegiance and commitment of members and the stronger the organization. The strength of union groups would therefore depend in large measure upon *how* important their collective functions are to members (how much power those functions have to stimulate membership participation and involvement). An additional factor is that although a member may become involved in a group and participate to the extent that he receives important satisfaction from the rewards of mere belonging, in most cases he will participate to the extent that he receives satisfaction from the act of participation itself. We suggest that the problem of inactive membership in the local unions studied resulted from the insufficient satisfaction the members received from either belonging or participating.

What does the evidence imply concerning the level of satisfaction local union members were receiving from participation? Within the locals of the present study, possibilities for meaningful participation consisted of holding office, serving on committees, attending meetings, voting, and communicating through formal or informal channels. We found that only a very few members held office, served on committees, or attended meetings; communication channels were woefully inadequate. The only form of participation practiced to any significant degree was voting. Although the opportunity to vote probably provides a certain amount of satisfaction as an act of participation, it would not seem enough to stimulate the kind of strength and cohesiveness necessary to provide a solution to the leadership problem.

Members obviously cannot receive satisfaction from participation unless there is an opportunity to participate. Even if there is an opportunity, they are not likely to participate unless they feel they are receiving meaningful satisfactions from their membership alone. It is likely that a significantly large percentage of the union membership studied were not receiving sufficient satisfactions from their membership alone. Local officers today are caught in a dilemma: members will not participate if they do not receive sufficient satisfaction from their membership; they will not receive such satisfaction unless they do participate.

We have sometimes implied and other times stated explicitly that satisfactions to be derived from the mere act of belonging to unions may not be as great as they once were. Satisfactions members receive from union affiliation depend upon what members want and how well unions fulfil what they want. In several foregoing sections, we have alluded to certain changes in the wants, desires, and attitudes of union members which seem to have taken place in the past thirty years. The importance for the present problem is that if the wants of union members have changed, that which is necessary for unions to provide in order to satisfy their wants will also have changed. Have unions changed sufficiently to provide meaningful satisfactions for the wants of union members of the sixties? Or, having failed to change, are they providing satisfactions for wants that no longer are as pressing as they were fifteen to thirty years ago? If the latter is the case, one may derive additional understanding of the participation problem faced by the local union officers.

It would, of course, be difficult to prove that union members of the sixties possess different wants than did those of the thirties. There is, however, much support for the proposition that members have changed.[8] Rising incomes and near full employment, with accompanying material well-being, have almost certainly created a different union member today —a member who is more generally satisfied with his economic

---

[8]See Richard A. Lester, *As Unions Mature* (Princeton, N. J.: Princeton University Press, 1958); and Sidney Lens, *The Crisis of American Labor* (New York: Sagamore Press, 1959).

situation and his conditions of employment, possesses stronger feelings of economic equality, is somewhat more moderate in political philosophy, and is more concerned with leisure and recreation. Divisions between economic classes are not as sharply drawn. More people have opportunities to do more things and own more things than ever before. Whereas today it is not unusual for union members to have expensive hobbies —to golf, to water ski, to shoot—thirty years ago this was not a possibility. The fact is union members *are* better off than they ever have been; they *are* comfortable. Security has seemingly become a more dominant concern and wages a less dominant one. Findings of the present study support the contention that security is in the forefront of awareness of union members. It may be recalled, in fact, that the findings also indicated that union officers seemed to overestimate the relative extent to which their members were concerned with wages, rather than security.

Although the tendency of unions to emphasize issues of job security increasingly (and their trend toward grievance-centered unionism) may reflect implicit recognition of the changes in union members, it is questionable whether these trends meet the real problem. As stated above, unions have not been successful in providing a substantial amount of job security for members, and the protection of the grievance procedure is not a positive, engaging type of satisfaction. It seems that what unions can provide in the way of security, wages, working conditions, and grievance-handling, although important, does not excite a large percentage of today's union members sufficiently to stimulate their active commitment to their organizations. Something more is needed to provide the kinds of satisfactions which will create participation and vitality in unions.

We are suggesting that the goals and structure of local unions will have to change to accommodate the changing wants of members if the foundation of unionism is to be stable and durable. Unions cannot return to the "good old days of the thirties" for many reasons, not the least of which is that their members are not the members of the thirties; nor can they hope to stimulate vitality in the present with goals and practices which do not appeal to their present membership. In essence, the failure of leadership which we have cited is more basically the failure of union organizations. However, if change is to take place, it will have to originate with the leadership and, to be most effective, will have to originate substantially with *local* union leadership, because of their closeness to the rank and file. This study has shown the extent to which local union members consider their organizations to be truly local organizations. Under such circumstances, only local union officers are in a position to exert influence to effect a meaningful change.

In order to enhance their success as leaders, officers will have to look at their problems in a new way. They will have to think about changing the structure and goals of their local unions, along with changing the orientation of their union members. The present emphasis upon substantially changing the characteristics of union members is a questionable, as well as an impossible, approach in a democratic context. The most reasonable solution is for union leaders to enlighten their members as to the facts of group and organizational life, insofar as this is practical and proper, and to seek positive changes in the structure of their organizations—changes which more adequately meet the needs of their members, thereby creating a more favorable context for participation and organizational success.

A starting point is to consider what union members *do* want. Although we have said that certain wants seem to be less important than they once were, nothing has been said about other wants which might be important but not adequately served. Increasing numbers of social critics, as well as students of society and management, have been pointing out that if there are any needs of workers today which probably are going unfulfilled, those needs are recognition and self-expression.[9] The literature of the "human relations" approach to management includes numerous discussions of the possibility for management to engage more fully the energies of workers through an appeal to their desire for self-expression. Among management policies under review are leadership practices of foremen, the structure of incentive systems, and the organization of work. The contention is that by concentrating on economic appeals to workers, management is ignoring an untapped source of energy based on a different set of wants—those for social recognition, creativity, and self-expression. Union organizations could well consider whether they might not also be ignoring such wants.

A particularly persuasive argument can be made that desires of workers for recognition, creativity, and self-expression are important at present, and perhaps much more so than they were in the not-too-distant past. The argument is based on a well-accepted notion concerning the nature of human motives: as an individual satisfies his basic desires (those for food, shelter, safety, rest), other "higher order" wants become relatively more important to him.[10] These "higher order" wants include social recognition, creativity, and self-expres-

---

[9]See such various sources as Frederick Herzberg, Bernard Mausner, and Barbara Snyderman, *The Motivation to Work* (New York: John Wiley and Sons, 1959); Chris Argyris, *Personality and Organization* (New York: Harper and Bros., 1957); Erich Fromm, *The Sane Society* (New York: Rinehart, 1955); Daniel Katz, "Satisfactions and Deprivations in Industrial Life," in Arthur Kornhouser, Robert Dubin, and Arthur M. Ross (eds.), *Industrial Conflict* (New York: McGraw-Hill Book Co., 1954); Douglas McGregor, *The Human Side of Enterprise* (New York: McGraw-Hill Book Co., 1960).

[10]Abraham H. Maslow, *Motivation and Personality* (New York: Harper and Bros., 1954).

sion. In other words, a worker whose thoughts are consumed in seeking the wages and working conditions necessary to provide the basic essentials for himself and his family is not likely to be driven by needs for creativity or self-expression. Needs for self-expression may be released and become important, however, when such concerns are no longer dominant.

Ability to satisfy basic wants is, of course, related to economic well-being. Satisfaction of higher order wants may also be related in part to economic well-being, but it is also related to having a voice in matters that affect one, expressing abilities and interests, respecting oneself, and being respected by others. Unions offer satisfaction of basic wants through their emphasis on wages, working conditions, and security. However, as basic needs reach high levels of satisfaction, they become relatively less important, and union members today are having considerable success in satisfying many of these needs. The question which presses for an answer is: To what extent do unions provide their members with meaningful opportunities to satisfy "higher order" wants? The data of the present study indicate that the active core of local union members probably receive such satisfaction; the vast number of rank-and-file members does not.

The active core of union members receives satisfaction of higher order wants because they participate. Active, meaningful participation in an organization is a highly efficient way to express one's self, to be creative, and to achieve recognition and feelings of personal worth. For many active unionists, it is probably true that the more they participate, the more satisfaction they receive; the more satisfaction they receive, the more they participate. There is an intimate relationship between participation and the satisfaction of higher order wants; further, the obvious way for a union to provide members with satisfaction of higher order wants is to get them to participate. In effect, then, one chief way that unions can appeal to workers today and become a more functional and significant force in the lives of their members is to provide an organizational structure which makes it possible for more members to participate readily. Unions can attempt to appeal to more members by providing more of what we have termed the "internal" rewards of group membership.[11]

Solution of the participation problem which the local union officers perceive would have far-reaching ramifications. Such solution would not only remove an obstacle to the achievement of local union goals but in itself actually would constitute achievement of an important goal. To achieve such results, participation would have to be defined as more than attendance at meetings, however. In reality, large numbers of members attending local union meetings might do nothing but create confusion, inefficiency, and dissatisfaction. Local union meetings probably will be dominated by more articulate members. It may be more frustrating to higher order wants to attend a meeting and not be able to participate than not to attend at all. Union meetings serve an important and well-recognized function, but they are probably not the most appropriate vehicle for meaningful participation by large numbers of members. To be successful as leaders, local union officers may have to devise alternate means of participation through which more members may more regularly achieve the satisfaction which stems from self-expression and feelings of personal worth.

A simple and potentially rewarding point from which to start would be the improvement of communications systems in local unions. Not only could more effective means be devised to keep members informed, but more members could be afforded the opportunity to express their opinions and

---

[11]George Homans, *The Human Group* (New York: Harcourt, Brace and Co., 1950).

suggestions through structured, efficient channels of communications. Such channels would have to be woven into the day-to-day activities of union members. They would have to be easy to use, and members would have to be encouraged to use them without fear of recrimination. Implementation of such a communications scheme might properly become a subject for collective bargaining. Management might make provision for workers to spend the small amounts of time away from jobs that might be necessary to make their opinions concerning union affairs known to a representative.

There is no reason why subjects of discussion need be confined to the world of work. As representatives of workers' special interests, unions provide a unique means by which their members might also express themselves on what concerns them in the spheres of community and national affairs.

A major requirement for the success of such a system would be that the participation be meaningful: members would have to feel their opinions were desired and did count. With participation would have to come a certain amount of control. Satisfying participation includes more than the mere formality of attending meetings or expressing opinions: it includes the feeling that one's presence is important, or that one's opinion is vital; it must also include the feeling that the power to exert *some* influence is a realistic possibility. Findings of this study have indicated that substantially high degrees of membership control are not damaging to successful leadership. The study did not make clear, however, that among local union officers, desires for greater membership participation necessarily imply desires for greater membership control. In some local unions, successful participation may require that officers share a greater degree of control over organizational matters with members.

Still other means for local unions to provide for greater satisfaction of members' higher order wants include: more imagi-

native use of stewards as closer links between the rank and
file and the leadership; greater use of referendums and questionnaires; and a broadened committee system with responsibilities for dealing with affairs of concern to workers outside,
as well as inside, the industrial plant. Another might be for
unions to provide broadened educational programs of appeal
to the special interests of their members.[12]

All these means of improving the ability of local unions to
serve the higher order wants of their members should have
the effect of tying more members more intimately to their
organization and should promote increased morale, integration, efficiency, and power, leading to increased ability of the
union to achieve still more satisfactions for members (namely,
those which accrue from the rewards of merely belonging—
the "external" rewards of membership.)[13] Traditionally, the
external rewards of union membership have been those which
stem from successful attainment of goals of wages, working
conditions, and security.

The nature of the external rewards of unionism also may
have to be reassessed in view of the changing characteristics
of union members. Wages and working conditions (as traditionally conceived) probably are relatively less important
to union members than they once were. Other goals which
can be achieved through bargaining or effective political
action may be becoming relatively more important. If this is
so, union officers will have to be more flexible and imaginative

---

[12]Local unions, either singly or united with others, could be far
more energetic in establishing training and education programs for their
members, and even the members' families. Our experience in Ohio has
demonstrated that many members are eager for relatively inexpensive
opportunities to further their own skills and educational backgrounds.
While considerable opportunities are already provided by community
and other groups, either members don't know about them or believe
they are not intended for workers but, instead, are meant for the
"middle class."

[13]Homans, op. cit.

in their approach to the bread-and-butter goals of unionism. For example, although automation is increasingly on the minds of union members, few unions have shown ingenuity in meeting the problem. Trends toward earlier retirement and the depersonalization of work create problems which fall into the same category. Still other issues may provide possibilities for creative approaches in specific situations.

Successful local union leadership will have to be increasingly concerned with whether union organizations meet adequately the new challenges of our industrial society. Since local officers are closest to members, they are in an advantageous position to assess the changing wants of members. Our findings have not indicated that officers perform this function well. They fail to perform it well, partly because they apparently find it difficult to break the bonds of tradition. They also fail to perform it well because of poor communications with members and because of the limited horizons of the officers. If dissatisfied, members can and do communicate by voting officers out of office; but that does not solve the problem. An additional difficulty resides in the inability of members to articulate adequately their aims, frustrations, and dissatisfactions, even if given the opportunity. Under such circumstances, members react to their unions in the only way they know—by demanding more personal services from officers.

The successful local union officer will be the one who leads by helping to articulate and set goals for members. To lead in this way local union officers will have to be perceptive of change, flexible in approach to unionism, and possessed of ability to withstand membership pressures while exerting positive influence on members in return.

In sum, it seems to us that the major task which faces local union leadership today is to make unionism a more positive force in the lives of union members. Success in local union leadership will not be easy to achieve; many problems will have to be surmounted.

Centralization of collective bargaining, discussed earlier, is one of these problems. Possibilities of reversing the trend to centralization, even if desirable, seem remote. If some way of providing union members with a more meaningful voice in the bargaining function cannot be found, participation in local union affairs is unlikely to be easily made more meaningful.

Another problem which will have to be met is the extent to which the time of local union officers is dominated by personal service and caretaking functions. The kind of creative leadership we have been discussing will require that the top local union officers be freed of the responsibilities of dealing with the personal problems of members. Although it is difficult within the democratic political structure of the local union, top officers must delegate these responsibilities more effectively to lesser officers, stewards, or committees. This could not be done easily without alienating a sizeable number of members. Our evidence indicates, however, that strong officers, operating within a well-structured organization, can accomplish such delegation successfully.

One additional problem which will have to be faced is the education of local union officers themselves. One of the reasons the local union members of the study did not participate in their organizations was their limited vision as to what unions stand for and what they could stand for. The limitation in the vision of members was, in significant respects, a reflection of the limited vision of the officers. Union members are not likely to change if their officers do not change; we believe members basically come to know their unions through their officers. Local union officers will thus not only have to acquire specific skills but also broaden their conception of unionism. Accordingly, some way must be found to educate local union officers effectively. Officers in turn may arouse members through a fresh approach to the responsibilties of their offices. The education of local union officers is sufficiently important to warrant separate discussion.

Implications of the Findings for Labor Education

IN PRECEDING SECTIONS, it has been reported that many of the officers of the five locals do not demonstrate a high degree of leadership as that term is used in this study. Many seem to be incapable of viewing their union and unionism in general in any other way than that which has become traditional. They fail to perceive alternative union-member relationships, fail to visualize the relationship between the local union and the larger society of which it is a part, and fail also to understand the relationship of social, economic, and political changes to their own unions. Beset by numerous (though not necessarily unimportant) membership demands, they lack the critical ability to forge new structures and relationships that could contain the performance of necessary, more-or-less routine functions and that could, consequently, give them the free time that might make possible their emergence as leaders. Although such free time is a necessary condition for the development of leadership attributes, alone it is not sufficient. Also highly desirable is their exposure to, and conditioning by, planned education programs.

The demands placed upon local union officers require a high degree of interpersonal skills for dealing with union members, as well as specific skills necessary for dealing with the employer. They also require the specialized organizational skills that are necessary to structure and maintain efficient organization. These demands are imposing. Most local officers are bound by long-standing traditional concepts and methods of behavior that are detached from social, political, and economic reality; it is imperative that alternative concepts and behavior be considered and evaluated. This process requires insight into the workings of society and its components as well as the twin abilities to consider relationships abstractly and reach appropriate judgments. Whereas organizational skills and skills necessary for effective interpersonal and employer relationships can be acquired through experience by the astute officer, if necessary, the development of intellectual skills and concepts usually requires the supplementation of experience by the advice, guidance, and counsel seldom available apart from formal education. The acquisition of the other skills is also facilitated by formal education, as compared to acquisition through unplanned experience.

The skills required for the emergence of leadership in union organizations are not uniquely associated with union organizations. They would be required for leadership in any organization. However, compared to most other organizations in America, the education that is prerequisite for this function is less in evidence in union locals. Data already presented verify comparatively low levels of formal education achieved by local union members and officers. Moreover, many of the officers we contacted said they were forced to learn their union duties through experience combined with help from other officers and international representatives. National and international union headquarters have long been cognizant of the need to fill the educational vacuum created by the workers' educational deficiencies. Working independently or with universities and other public institutions, they have tried to provide educational opportunities for workers in general. They have also expended considerable energy in establishing educational programs that are designed to satisfy their institutional needs. These programs have, by now, formed certain patterns. Commenting on the emphasis of university worker-education programs Jack Barbash observes:

. . . The dominant emphasis has been on the "bread-and-butter" subjects like steward training, collective bargaining, public speaking, and parliamentary law, union administration, etc. This emphasis stems largely from the nature of union demand for vocationally competent union officers.[14]

---

[14]Jack Barbash, *Universities and Unions in Workers' Education* (New York: Harper and Bros., 1955), p. 8.

Additionally, however, international and local unions have co-operated with universities and colleges in presenting programs dealing with social problems; other programs have been designed that center upon instruction in the social sciences and humanities. All in all, unions and co-operating universities and colleges have approached the objective of classroom education from many different routes. Their failures to attract widespread participation and exert meaningful impact upon unionism at the local level are well known; the findings of this study similarly demonstrate that the officers of the five locals generally lack the education that would make the greatest contribution to their growth as union leaders. At the same time, almost all of them have participated in such education programs as short courses and summer institutes. Also, they have occasional access to other educational instruments. Among these are international representatives, various union publications such as newspapers and magazines, and other AFL-CIO courses designed for specific problems. Whether or not the educational opportunities have furthered the "vocational competence" of these local officers, the programs have not provided adequate opportunities for their leadership development.

For the most part, education programs made available to local union officers by various levels of the international union stress improving the officers' abilities to function efficiently in the performance of various routinized tasks. From the international's point of view, this is a step required by the growth of unions into large, complex organizations that need co-ordination to avoid dissipation of power. Local officers must receive training leading to the efficient performance of the routine duties embodied in their offices, but this type of training is inadequate to insure the organizational health of the union.

Many members (perhaps *most* of the members) in the five local unions have none or few of the characteristics of a union group or organization. This large proportion of the members

pays its dues and expects certain services to be provided by
the officers, either on schedule or on call. Beyond this minimal
attachment, these members are not union members. From this
it follows that the unions can regularly be expected to perform
certain given functions and no others, even in the face of
various environmental changes that might require organizational modifications and adaptations in order to protect the
welfare of all the members. This is obviously a sign of lack
of organization that might presently, or in the near future,
lead to organizational impotence. Vocational education is inadequate to insure the organizational health of the union
because it is meaningful only if the organization is healthy.
If the great majorities of members do not attend meetings, or
otherwise congregate together, what is the organizational
importance of parliamentary procedure or public speaking?
In a superficial sense, the failure of leadership by officers of
the five locals results from their lack of followers: they have
few members to lead, but many to "service."

Although "clients" are easier to come by than either leaders
or followers, their loyalties and attachments are more a
function of economics than of dedication to ideals and causes.
But unions in America have been built upon the proposition,
which they constantly reaffirm, that they are a movement
intended to advance the cause of social justice. Almost any
union constitution makes such claims. If this really is desired,
then it is incumbent upon union leaders to begin their quest
for union followers. This condition, however, is unrecognized
(for the most part) by the union officers we have studied.
Although their sincerity is unquestioned and although they
seemingly possess innate intelligence, the officers we have
studied would likely begin their work in constructing a group
by "making the meetings shorter and keeping out hard ideas
that are confusing."

It is our judgment that leadership training is training in
the social sciences and the humanities and that union officers

require such training or education if they are to assume positions of leadership in a social movement or organization. If they are solely to be providers of services, this judgment does not apply. On the other hand, it does apply if they are to provide necessary services while also constructing organizational components of a social movement. In addition, they would also require vocational training, but the allocation between vocational and leadership training must be of an optimum nature, since their vocational and leadership successes would be interdependent in nature. The social sciences and humanities are well suited to provide that which is most desperately needed for leadership: knowledge of institutions, relationships and interdependencies within society, knowledge of alternative societal arrangements and their implications, and insights into the forces which motivate people.

In addition to the social science-humanities content of the education program for leaders, the program itself must be long-term in nature. Despite the popularity of gimmicks and short cuts, no one has yet devised a successful method of transplanting the ideas of, say, economics, sociology, or philosophy from teacher to student during a weekend or a few hours one night a week for six, eight, or ten weeks.

For the most part, the kinds of programs advocated for educating officers so they might function as leaders are not commonly found in the American labor scene. There are several obvious reasons for this. In the first place, long-term programs require heavy investments in the participants. If the participants are union officers, and if the program is scheduled over, say, a three- or four-year period, the participants may fail to win elections and, hence, lose their official positions. In that event, the union (if it is paying for the programs) would find itself in the position either of continuing members in leadership training programs who are no longer officers or withdrawing the participants without offices and replacing them with the new officers. If the unions are inclined toward the latter course, they might find that despite substantial expenditures over a period of years none of their members have completed the entire program. In this case the returns would not justify the cost. On the other hand, convincing the membership that the union should keep members who have lost their offices in the leadership programs described also would be difficult in the usual case.

Another reason why programs of the social science–humanities type probably have not appeared has already been mentioned: unions have perceived their first need to be vocational training for officers and activists. Accordingly, such educational instruments as short courses, conferences, and institutes (held both on and off university campuses) have been utilized for this purpose. In addition to their educational value, these courses sometimes serve an entirely different function—providing rewards for "deserving" officers and activists. Some of these programs, lasting from several days to a week or longer, are held in locations other than the hometowns of many of the participants, thus giving them the opportunity for "seeing something different." Since the participants frequently receive income from the union compensating them for time lost on the job, as well as fairly liberal room accommodations, food, and travel allowances, the programs probably take on the flavor of an added vacation. If some labor-education programs are viewed in this manner, they may be a firmly entrenched, if latent, part of a union's reward and punishment system. As such, they would be difficult to dislodge even though they may have the consequence of absorbing a sufficiently large proportion of a union's education budget to preclude the development of different types of programs. This is not to say that these programs are not worth their cost. In addition to whatever vocational and other training is accomplished and serving also as a means of rewarding good organizational performances, the programs are useful in bringing together union members and permitting them to develop group loyalties and attachments. Bringing together union officers from different states, different communities within a state, or different locals within a community provides a forum for demonstrating that they belong to an organization that is large (and, by implication, powerful) and composed of people who have ideas, values, and problems in common. While such programs might be reflective of leadership acts, they do not of themselves necessarily produce leadership in any systematic fashion.

Still another reason why labor-education programs tend to be short-term and vocational in nature is that these programs can best utilize the capabilities of the educational staff of the international unions. Despite some co-operation from universities, colleges, and other public or quasi-public agencies, unions continue to plan, promote, and execute many, if not most, labor-education programs. This condition requires them to maintain staff personnel who can be dispatched to almost any part of the United States in order to carry out a program thought to be feasible and desirable. Nevertheless, the individual international union's capabilities are such that only programs that are comparatively short and that fall within the competence of a fairly small number of people can be attempted. Certainly it is obvious that the education programs that seem to be most suitable for the systematic development of labor leaders are beyond the capacities of the international unions acting individually. Such programs, stretching across a band described by the terms "social sciences" and the "humanities," although perhaps dependent upon the latter to a lesser extent, require instructional capabilities that only colleges and universities usually possess.

Development of leadership training programs requires a higher degree of co-operation between universities and colleges and the unions. Such a relationship needs to be free of certain difficulties that have arisen in the past between union and university educators. For instance, in the past either union or university educators have attempted to dominate the relationship. While this may be an inevitable human tendency, it is nevertheless dysfunctional. University and labor union educators have distinctly different roles, for the performance of which each has certain obvious advantages. The university educators have or should have more breadth of experience in dealing with such matters as curricula, methods of instruction appropriate for the curricula, the actual instruction, and preparation of course materials. The university or college usually does not have physical or intellectual access to local union officers such that it could efficiently instil in them the value of long-term, liberal education. Further, it might be argued that even if the schools did have this access, it is not their proper role to "sell" education on the required levels and scales. It would seem, therefore, that the proper and efficient role of the union educator is that of building awareness about, and interest in, leadership programs that, in turn, can be offered by the schools. However, if the relationship between union and university educators fails to be broadened and extended to that required for the implementation of a leadership program, neither unions nor schools can make the contribution of which they are capable to the existence of a democratic society.

Among other things, one of the conclusions of this study is that relatively few of the local union members possess anything like a social-movement philosophy. It is likely that this finding will not be the source of much surprise, since it is commonplace today to hear and read arguments that unions must acquire such a philosophy if they are to maintain, if not expand, their spheres and degrees of influence. It is our belief that the issue underlying these arguments is, not the specific directions in which unionism should proceed, but the members' lack of strongly felt goals and interdependencies, which ultimately might prevent unionism from going anywhere at all.

It was suggested above that unions acquire their power and influence in the larger society from the extent to which their members are willing to contribute their energies and support to the organization. In turn, the data show that many members fall into such commonly used categories as "apathetic" and "disinterested:" it is clear that many members do not possess a philosophy (a system of looking at and guiding life) that ranks the labor union high in its system of values. Therefore, one may say logically that if more of the members possessed a union philosophy, unions would be stronger, more influential instrumentalities. Unfortunately, however, many of those who are either working within the unions or are studying and analyzing union activities and who cry the need for a union philosophy in order to make unions stronger conclude that such a philosophy must be taught to the members. The stress upon the need for instilling this philosophy presupposes that such a philosophy actually exists, that it can be taught, and that, once taught, members would use it to order and guide their lives.

The existence of a union-movement philosophy seldom has been identifiable in the history of American unionism, apart from its existence among the corps of union professionals and a few others. Moreover, philosophy, even when its terms and concepts have been carefully worked out, usually cannot be transferred from one person to another with as much facility as, say, labor law or the principles of collective bargaining. A philosophy of life seems to be acquired as the outcome of lifelong experiences and interpersonal relationships. For this reason, it seems reasonable to postulate that attempts to alter the philosophies of people generally will be unsuccessful unless they rely heavily upon life experiences and interpersonal relationships. Though formal education is a form of both experience and interpersonal relationship, it is not likely that short courses or even liberal, long-term education programs can, by themselves, be efficient instruments for the

development of a meaningful philosophy for large numbers
of union members—if for no other reason than education is
not that highly valued by most members. Thus, it appears
that if members' philosophies are to be altered to correspond
more nearly to a social movement–union type, it must be as
the outcome of leadership itself.

7. A Final Comment

THIS MANUSCRIPT has cast doubt and offered criticism throughout as to the quality of leadership in local unions as exemplified by the practices found in five local unions studied in Columbus, Ohio. The criticism leveled should not be interpreted as that of unfriendly persons looking for issues to raise or critical points to make. Rather, it reflects the judgment drawn from a hopefully unprejudiced effort to examine the quality of leadership found in local unions.

The findings which we have reported cannot be regarded as reassuring; neither should they be regarded as suggesting that the death knell of trade-unions is about to sound. Rather, the judgment is that clearly major problems exist and that there is need for improved leadership. Our study of local unions sprang from the preconception that the local union must continue to be a major segment of union structure; these preconceptions were confirmed. Even though the negotiation of basic contracts may shift more and more from the local to higher echelons of unions, the administration of the agreement must reside largely with the local. Similarly, and equally or more important, the building of group cohesion must be achieved largely in the local. Here is the spot where genuine personal participation and involvement can be exercised, and here is where the great bulk of organizational leadership must be exercised. The unfortunate tendency of recent years—to downgrade the local union as a major echelon of the union movement—must be reversed if a functionally democratic union movement is to be maintained or re-established in the United States.

In the 1960's, critics of the union movement are numerous. Not only the critics found among business organizations, the academic world, and legislative bodies are voicing criticism; but also, erstwhile friends of unions are complaining about the failure of unions.[1]

If unions are to be meaningful and helpful to their members, there can be little question that the union movement today must undertake a thorough re-evaluation of its total structure and goals, viewed especially in the light of changing economic and social conditions and a rapidly changing technology. Certainly, many of the criticisms by friends of unionism are primarily the complaints of persons who see a need in modern society for an organization, such as a union, to aid individuals in meeting economic, sociological, psychological, and political problems which are beyond their power (and perhaps understanding). Our judgment is that many of the issues facing the union movement today also are difficult to grasp for local union leadership as it now is constituted.

Yet, the problems of union members must be met, in part at least, by their organizations if the organizations are to continue to be effective as voluntary groups; and the issues must be solved in good part at the local level. Membership attendance at meetings, willingness to serve on committees, interest in the welfare of other members as well as one's self, knowledge and support of union goals and policies, and many other elements of genuine member participation can be developed only at the local union level.

---

[1]See, for example, Paul Jacobs, *The State of the Union,* (New York: Atheneum Publishers, 1963); Solomon Barkin, *The Decline of the Labor Movement* (New York: Fund for the Republic, 1962); and "The Crisis in the American Trade Union Movement," *The Annals of the American Academy of Political and Social Science,* XXXL, November, 1963.

It seems likely that these can be developed at the local union level only with a higher caliber of leadership than presently exists. This is why the expensive and time-consuming task of widespread, broad-based union leadership education programs might usefully be undertaken. Without question, certain personal characteristics of leadership may be developed through experience. But it is suggested that, given the formal educational attainment of the typical union officer, additional educational experience and broadly-based learning opportunities must be accorded if the local is not to become a less and less significant division of the union movement— keeping records, answering correspondence, and performing other routine functions. If the quality of local union leadership is not improved, and if the industrial, sociological, and psychological world in which local unions operate continues to grow more complex, then of necessity the local union will become less important. If so, democratic unionism, both real and potential, also declines.

It is in the firm belief that the union movement, as a major bulwark of practicing economic and political democracy, must be reinvigorated that our strong and sometimes severe criticism of local unionism is made.

Appendixes

A. The Method of the Study

THE DATA FOR THIS STUDY were collected from five local unions in a medium-sized midwestern city—Columbus, Ohio. Each of the five local unions had between four hundred and seven hundred members at the time the study was undertaken, and each of them is organized along industrial lines. Their employers are all manufacturing firms. The local unions were chosen in consultation with international union officials in accordance with predetermined criteria of size, industry type, and sex and occupational characteristics of members. Complete co-operation of the internationals was obtained in each case. The influence of the internationals was particularly valuable in gaining introduction to the locals.

Because of the nature of the study, it was necessary to identify two different sources of data—the officers and the members. Although the definition of local union officers may vary for different purposes, we decided to define them as all of the members of each executive board. Thus, while we did not include such officials as stewards, our definition embraces all of the local-wide officers such as president, secretaries, financial-secretaries, and the like. All the members of the executive boards were elected to their positions by local-wide elections. As a result of board vacancies and differences in bylaws, the size of the executive boards of the different locals varied between six and nine members. As a preliminary step, the authors of the study met personally with the executive boards of each of the five locals. The nature and purposes of the study were explained and the co-operation of the boards was sought. Interest among board members was high, and excellent co-operation was attained.

Each of the members of the executive boards was interviewed at length. Choice of questions employed in the interviews was guided by the purposes and conceptual outline of the study. The questions were general in nature, and the board members were encouraged to respond in any manner they believed appropriate. Questions employed in the interview schedules were tested in advance on other local union officers not connected with any of the five local unions included in this study. The major part of the pretest procedure consisted of reducing the numbers of questions, as it was discovered that the officers' answers were quite expansive. The interviews of the officers in the five sample unions lasted between approximately two and five hours each and, in some cases, required several different meetings. None of the officers refused to co-operate; complete interviews were obtained from each of the total of forty-one. The interviewers believe they received frank expressions of opinion.

Both interview and questionnaire techniques were used in studying the members of the five locals. The first step was preparation of an interview schedule of questions which seemed appropriate with the conceptual outline of the study. The schedule was tested and revised several times on the basis of experience with it in interviewing a number of members from local unions other than the five studied. Approximately twenty members from each of the five unions were selected randomly for interviews from rosters of members provided by the executive boards. Again, the questions employed were fairly general. These members were also found to be co-operative and frank. The durations of their interviews varied between one to two hours. Out of ninety-three members selected for interviews, sixty-six (or approximately 71 per cent), were actually interviewed; nineteen refused interviews for various reasons, and eight could not be located. During the early stages of the interviewing, it was discovered that the membership rosters contained addresses for members which frequently were incorrect. In some cases, members had moved without giving their union a new address. Some of the house numbers were incorrect, and streets spelled similarly were sometimes confused. This deficiency proved to be extremely troublesome during the data-collection phases of the study.

The interviews with members had several different objectives. One was to provide a guide for the construction of the questionnaires. For example, the categories of answers used in the questionnaires were almost all derived from responses obtained in the interviews. Since we attempted to construct the questionnaires in terms the members themselves used and understood, the response to the questions asked during the interviews, as well as the interviewers' experiences in phrasing the questions, were invaluable guides. Another objective of the interviews was to collect types of data which, as a practical matter, could not be obtained by questionnaire. The interviews also proved to be valuable guides and references for the interpretation of data obtained by questionnaire.

Samples of members to be sent questionnaires were drawn randomly from the membership rosters previously mentioned. Members selected for interviews were excluded from these samples. Approximately one out of seven members in each of the locals was selected to receive a questionnaire. The questionnaire itself was intended to collect information from large numbers of members: adequate sampling demanded inclusion of more members in the study than we had resources to interview. The questionnaire was designed to elicit information comparable to that obtained by interview and was modeled in accordance with the basic conceptual scheme of the study.

For the most part, the questionnaires were distributed by mailing them to the members. In some cases, however, they were distributed by union stewards or research project staff members. All the questionnaires were returned to the research staff through the mails.

A total of 457 questionnaires was distributed to members of the five locals. The initial response was somewhat disappointing, as only 164 (or 36 per cent) of these questionnaires were returned in usable form. Although the response rate was low, it was not unexpected. It was necessary to distribute most of the questionnaires by mail, using addresses supplied by the local unions. As explained above, the addresses were frequently incorrect. Whereas we had adequate resources to track down the addresses of small numbers of members, our resources were inadequate to do this for the larger numbers included in the samples receiving questionnaires. Approximately 40 per cent of the questionnaires sent out in the initial mailing were returned as undeliverable. The use of telephone directories and city directories helped to increase the number ultimately delivered, but it is believed that approximately 20 per cent of them failed to reach the persons for whom they were intended.

Accordingly, small samples from each local were drawn randomly from the lists of members who failed to return usable questionnaires. A total sample of eighty-nine non-respondents was thus selected and followed up after extensive and costly efforts were made to determine their addresses. Most of the members included in this sample were contacted personally by members of the research staff. Approximately 70 per cent returned usable questionnaires, although again, a few refused to co-operate and a few could not be located at all. Adding these follow-ups to the questionnaires originally returned brought the final total of respondents to 227, or approximately 50 per cent of the original sample of members.

Comparisons of the attitudes and characteristics of the original respondent group and the follow-up group failed to reveal significant differences between them. Thus, we concluded that on the basis of everything known, both the original and follow-up groups approximately represented the total membership in each of the local unions. On the strength of limited information obtained about those people who refused to return questionnaires when contacted personally or who refused to be interviewed, it was concluded that these groups probably would not be the cause of systematic bias in the study.

All in all, in our judgment the distributions of characteristics and attitudes obtained in the course of this study are representative of the entire membership of the five local unions.

B. Union Member Questionnaire

DIRECTIONS: Please indicate your answers by placing check marks in the appropriate spaces.

Questions about Your Background as a Union Member

1. How many years have you been a member of your local union?

less than 1	1–2	3–4	5–9	10–19	20 or more

2. What is the total number of years you have been a union member?

less than 1	1–2	3–4	5–9	10–19	20 or more

3. Are you now a steward or other officer in your local union?

yes	no

If your answer is yes, what position do you hold? (Write in answer.)

_____

4. Have you been an officer in your local union in the past year?

_____   _____

yes   **no**

5. Are you now on any union committees?   _____   _____

yes   no

6. Have you been on any union committees in the past?

_____   _____

yes   no

7. About how many regularly scheduled local union meetings have you attended during the last twelve months?   _____

8. About how many special meetings of your local union have you attended during the last twelve months?   _____

9. Did you vote in the last local union election of officers?

_____   _____

yes   **no**

10. What would you say is your chief source of news about local union affairs?

A. ___ attending local union meetings

B. ___ talking with stewards

C. ___ talking with other union members

D. ___ talking with top local union officers

E. ___ reading the bulletin board

F. ___ reading notices and the mail

G. ___ **none**

H. ___ other (Write in answer.)

11. Do you read the union paper regularly? _____   _____
                                                              yes   no

12. Other than your union do you belong to any other organiza-
    tion? _____   _____
           yes   **no**

    If you do belong to other organizations, to how many do you
    belong? _____

Questions about Your Union

13. How much do you think the membership has to say about
    how things are decided in your local union?

    _____   _____   _____   _____   _____
    a great deal   a fair amount   some   very little   no say at all

14. How much do you think the local president has to say about
    how things are decided in your local union?

    _____   _____   _____   _____   _____
    a great deal   a fair amount   some   very little   no say at all

15. How much do you think the executive board has to say about
    how things are decided in your local union?

    _____   _____   _____   _____   _____
    a great deal   a fair amount   some   very little   no say at all

16. How much do you think the bargaining committee has to say
    about how things are decided in your local union?

    _____   _____   _____   _____   _____
    a great deal   a fair amount   some   very little   no say at all

17. There are many different things a local union might try to get.
    Some of these things are listed below. We would like your

opinion on two separate matters for each thing listed. First, check yes or no whether you think your local *is* trying to get the thing. Second, check yes or no whether you think your local *should* be trying to get the thing. In other words, for each thing listed you should indicate with check marks your opinion on two separate matters.

	Is your local union trying to get the thing? (Check either yes, no, or don't know for each thing listed at left.)			*Should* your local union be trying to get the thing? (Check either yes, no, or don't know for each thing listed at left.)		
	yes	no	don't know	yes	no	don't know
A. Higher wages for workers	___	___	___	___	___	___
B. Better working conditions for workers	___	___	___	___	___	___
C. Protection for workers from management	___	___	___	___	___	___
D. More say in running the plant	___	___	___	___	___	___
E. Better health, pension, and insurance benefits for workers	___	___	___	___	___	___

		Is your local union trying to get the thing? (Check either yes, no, or don't know for each thing listed at left.)			Should your local union be trying to get the thing? (Check either yes, no, or don't know for each thing listed at left.)		
		yes	no	don't know	yes	no	don't know
F.	More job security for workers	—	—	—	—	—	—
G.	Better seniority plan	—	—	—	—	—	—
H.	Longer vacations and more holidays	—	—	—	—	—	—
I.	More social and recreational activities for workers	—	—	—	—	—	—
J.	A better life for all people in the community	—	—	—	—	—	—
K.	Equal rights for all workers	—	—	—	—	—	—
L.	More support for the aims of the international union	—	—	—	—	—	—
M.	More organizing of unorganized plants	—	—	—	—	—	—

	Is your local union trying to get the thing? (Check either yes, no, or don't know for each thing listed at left.)			*Should* your local union be trying to get the thing? (Check either yes, no, or don't know for each thing listed at left.)		
	yes	no	don't know	yes	no	don't know
N. More members interested in the local	——	——	——	——	——	——
O. Greater unity and strength in the local	——	——	——	——	——	——
P. More political action from members	——	——	——	——	——	——
Q. More members educated about union affairs	——	——	——	——	——	——
R. Other (write in)	——	——	——	——	——	——

Please write in the letter of the *one* thing you think is most important. _____

18. Do you think your top local union officers want your local to do the same things you want it to do?

——————   ——————   ——————
yes   no   don't know

19. How do you find out what things your top local union officers want your local to do? (Please check as many as apply.)

    A. __ I attend union meetings and hear it there.

    B. __ I find out from my steward.

    C. __ I read about what they want.

    D. __ I find out from other union members.

    E. __ I ask the top local union officers.

    F. __ The top officers make a point of telling me what they are after.

    G. __ I don't know what they want the local to do.

    H. __ other (Write in answer.)

---

20. Do you think your international union wants your local to do the same things you want it to do?

    ————   ————   ————————

    yes   no   don't know

21. How do you find out what things your international union wants your local union to do? (Please check as many as apply.)

    A. __ I attend union meetings and hear it there.

    B. __ I hear about it from my steward.

    C. __ I read about it in the union paper.

    D. __ I ask the top local union officers.

    E. __ The top officers make a point of telling me what the international wants.

F. ___ I hear about it from other union members.

G. ___ I ask the international representative.

H. ___ I don't know what it wants the local to do.

I. ___ other (Write in answer.)

---

22. There is usually more than one way to try to get a thing. What is the one best way your local union can use to try to get what it is after?

    A. ___ strike

    B. ___ demand them and threaten to strike

    C. ___ use political action

    D. ___ just bargain or talk it over with management

    E. ___ get more unity from local union members and put pressure on management

    F. ___ compromise with management

    G. ___ I don't know the best way

    H. ___ none of these methods is proper

    I. ___ other (Write in answer.)

---

23. Do you think your local union officers try to use the methods you have checked above?

    _____   _____   _____
    yes   no   don't know

24. Do you think political action helps unions get what they are
are after?

_____   _____   _____
   yes   no   don't know

25. Do you think it is proper for unions to use political action?

_____   _____   _____
   yes   no   don't know

26. Do you think there are any problems which stand in the way
of your local union's getting what it is after?

_____   _____   _____
   yes   no   don't know

If you have answered yes, check any of the following that
you think are problems for your local union. (Please check
as many as apply.)

A. ___ hard management to deal with

B. ___ bad public opinion concerning unions

C. ___ bad government laws concerning unions

D. ___ lack of interest on the part of local union members

E. ___ no unity in the local union

F. ___ poor local union officers

G. ___ too little help from the international union

H. ___ a few bad local union members

I. ___ I don't know what the problems are

J. ___ other (Please write in answer.)

27. How strong is your local union in getting what it goes after?

_____   _____   _____   _____
very strong   strong   neither strong nor weak   weak

_____
very weak

28. Which would you like to see your local union become?

_____   _____   _____
stronger   weaker   stay about same

29. If you had the power to change one condition which exists within your local union, which condition would you change if you wanted to benefit the local most? (Write in answer.)

_____

30. Do you know of anything your top local union officers have done to try to solve any of the problems of your local?

_____   _____
yes   no

If you do know of anything, please mention what was done. (Write in answer.)

_____

Was this action successful in helping to solve the problem?

_____   _____   _____
yes   no   don't know

31. What *one* thing do you think your top local union officers have to worry about most when they make an important decision? (Please check one.)

A. __ what the local union members will think

B. __ what the international union will think

C. __ what effect it will have on management

D. __ economic conditions

E. __ what effect it will have on public relations

F. __ I don't know what they have to worry about

G. __ other (Write in answer.)

---

32. Would you please mention any specific event that you know of in which a local union officer did an outstandingly good job for the union or an outstandingly bad job for the union. (Write in answer.)

---

33. What do you expect of the top elected officers of your local union? (Please check as many as apply.)

A. __ to be tough bargainers with management

B. __ to fight to win grievances

C. __ to run a democratic union meeting

D. __ to keep the local union members informed

E. __ to protect all the local union members all the time

F. __ to be honest and fair with local union members

G. __ to be honest and fair with management

H. __ to be leaders in the community

I. __ to do what local union members say

J. __ to get all they can out of management

K. ___ no strikes

L. ___ to compromise with management

M. ___ I don't know what I expect

N. ___ I don't expect anything

O. ___ other (Write in answer.)

Please write in the letter of the *one* thing you expect, that you think is most important. _____

34. How well do your local union officers live up to what you expect of them?

excellently	very well	neither well nor poorly	rather poorly	not at all

35. Do you think your local union officers face any problems which make it hard for them to live up to what you expect?

yes	no	don't know

36. How many hours per week would you guess your top local union officers spend on union business?

0–9	10–19	20–29	30–39	40–49	50 or more

37. What one type of union business would you guess takes the greatest amount of your top local union officers' time? (Please check one.)

A. ___ running union meetings

B. ___ keeping union records

  C. __ listening to local union members' grievances

  D. __ negotiating grievances with management

  E. __ negotiating contract with management

  F. __ discussing things with local union members

  G. __ discussing things with management

  H. __ attending union conferences and conventions

  I. __ discussing things with stewards and other local union officers

  J. __ writing letters and notices

  K. __ I don't know what takes their time

  L. __ other (Write in answer.)

---

38. Do you think you should actively participate in the affairs of your local union?

  ——————— ——————— ———————

   yes   no   don't know

39. What do you think your local union officers expect of you as a local union member? (Please check as many as apply.)

  A. __ attend union meetings

  B. __ back them up when they need help

  C. __ serve on union committees

  D. __ read the union paper

  E. __ vote in union elections

F. ___ keep informed about union affairs

G. ___ read the union contract

H. ___ co-operate with stewards

I. ___ they don't expect anything

J. ___ I don't know what they expect

K. ___ other (Write in answer).

_____

Do you think local union officers *should* expect these things of you?

_____   _____   _____

yes   no   don't know

If you have answered no, what do you think they *should* expect? (Write in answer.)

_____

40. How well do you think you live up to what the officers expect of you?

_____ _____ _____ _____ _____

excellently   very well   neither well   rather poorly   not at all
                            nor poorly

41. What satisfactions do you get out of belonging to your union? (Please check as many as apply.)

A. ___ I get satisfaction from a feeling of protection from the boss.

B. ___ I get satisfaction from a feeling of security.

C. ___ I get satisfaction from higher wages and better working conditions.

D. ___ I get satisfaction from feeling I am part of an important group.

E. ___ I get satisfaction from having good friends who are union brothers.

F. ___ I can help other members through the union.

G. ___ I get satisfaction from feeling I have more say about wages and conditions in the plant.

H. ___ I get satisfaction because I feel I learn from being part of the union.

I. ___ I don't get any satisfaction from the union.

J. ___ I don't know what satisfaction I get from the union.

K. ___ other (Write in answer.)

---

42. The union constitution grants union members certain rights. What are your rights as a union member? (Please check as many as apply.)

A. ___ right to vote in union elections

B. ___ right to hold union office

C. ___ right to speak out in the union on any subject

D. ___ right to file a grievance

E. ___ right to know how union funds are used

F. ___ right to bring charges against an unworthy union officer

G. ___ I don't know what my rights are

H. ___ I have no rights

I. ___ other (Write in answer.)

---

43. Do you feel your rights as a union member are protected in your local?

    _____   _____   _____
     yes   no   don't know

44. Do you think any group of members in your local union is being left out?

    _____   _____   _____
     yes   no   don't know

    If you have answered yes, what group do you feel is being left out? (Write in answer.)

---

45. What in general do you think your local union expects of your international union? (Please check as many as apply.)

    A. ___ to help out when requested by the local

    B. ___ to keep the local informed

    C. ___ to offer advice and suggestions about how the local should be run

    D. ___ to keep the local "in line" by telling the local what to do

    E. ___ to organize unorganized plants in the industry

    F. ___ I don't know what the local expects.

    G. ___ Nothing is expected.

    H. ___ other (Write in answer.)

---

46. How well do you think your international union lives up to what the local expects?

   _____ _____ _____ _____ _____
   excellently very well neither well rather poorly not at all
                          nor poorly

47. How much do you think your international union should have to say about how things are run in your local union?

   ___ everything to say

   ___ very much to say

   ___ a fair amount to say

   ___ very little to say

   ___ nothing to say

48. Do you think your local union has any obligation or responsibility to your international union?

   _____ _____ _____
   yes   no   don't know

   If you have answered yes, what is the obligation? (Please check as many as apply.)

   A. ___ support the international financially

   B. ___ keep the international informed

   C. ___ do what the international advises

   D. ___ listen to the suggestions of the international

   E. ___ help the international organize unorganized plants

   F. ___ I don't know what the obligation is.

   G. ___ other (Write in answer.)

49. Do you think your local union has any obligation or responsibility to your company?

——————— ——————— ———————
  yes   no   don't know

If you have answered yes, what is the obligation? (Please check as many as apply.)

A. ___ not to take away from profits

B. ___ not to make too many demands

C. ___ to be fair and square

D. ___ to make suggestions about how the company can improve itself

E. ___ decrease demands when necessary to keep company competitive

F. ___ help company compete by organizing unorganized plants

G. ___ let company run business without interference

H. ___ I don't know what the obligation is.

I. ___ other (Write in answer.)

---

50. Do you think unions in general have any obligation or responsibility to the general public?

——————— ——————— ———————
  yes   no   don't know

If you have answered yes, what is the obligation? (Please check as many as apply.)

A. __ to keep down prices by going slow on wage demands

B. __ to be a clean and honest organization

C. __ to be a democratic organization

D. __ to follow policies that will benefit the general public

E. __ to help out in charity drives and public-welfare programs

F. __ to inform the public

G. __ to organize the public

H. __ I don't know what the obligation is.

I. __ other (Write in answer.)

Some Questions of Opinion

51. Do you think anything should be done to prevent unemployment resulting from slack business conditions?

_____ _____
yes no

Do you think anything should be done to prevent unemployment resulting from automation?

_____ _____
yes no

52. Do you think the government can do anything to prevent unemployment resulting from slack business conditions?

_____ _____
yes no

Do you think the government can do anything to prevent unemployment resulting from automation?

_____   _____
  yes   no

53. Do you think the union can do anything to prevent unemployment resulting from slack business conditions?

_____   _____
  yes   no

Do you think the union can do anything to prevent unemployment resulting from automation?

_____   _____
  yes   no

54. How do you feel about your company as a place to work?

____ excellent—always treats workers extremely well

____ good—usually treats workers fairly and squarely

____ medium—neither good nor bad in treatment of workers

____ poor—makes things hard for workers

____ very bad—an extreme enemy of workers

Questions about You

55. Please indicate your sex. _____   _____
                                male   female

56. How old are you?

_____   _____   _____   _____   _____
under 20   20–29   30–39   40–49   50–59

_____
over 60

57. Please check the block below that indicates the amount of schooling you have had.

— — — — — — — —   Grade School
1 2 3 4 5 6 7 8

— — — —   High School
9 10 11 12

— — — —   College
13 14 15 16

58. Are you ———— ———— ——————————————?
            single   married   divorced, widowed, separated

59. Are you the chief source of income for your household?

———   ————
yes   no

60. How many dependents do you have other than yourself?

————   ————   ————
2 or less   3–5   6 or more

61. Are you employed at the present time?   ————   ————
                                                    yes   no

62. Please state briefly the title of your job and describe what you do in this job.   (Write in answer.)

_____

Is your job considered ————   ————   ————?
                        skilled   semiskilled   unskilled

63. Have you ever been in other occupations? ————   ————
                                                    yes   no

What other *chief* occupation have you had? (Write in answer.)

_____

64. If you are married, does your wife (husband) work?

_____   _____
  yes   no

Is your wife (husband) a union member? _____   _____
                                           yes   no

Does your wife (husband) approve of union activities?

_____   _____
  yes   no

65. What was your father's usual occupation? (Write in answer.)

_____

Was your father a union member? _____   _____
                                   yes   no

66. Have you ever been unemployed? _____   _____
                                     yes   no

Have you ever been unemployed for more than thirty days?

_____   _____
  yes   no

How many times have you been unemployed for more than thirty days?

_____

C. Interview Questions: Union Members

1. What do you think are the goals, or aims, of your local union? (What is your local after? What is it trying to do?)

   Should these be the aims of your local? If not, what should the aims of the local be?

2. What do you think your top local union officers want the local to accomplish? How do you find out what the officers want the local to accomplish?

3. What do you think your international union wants the local to accomplish? How do you know what the international wants the local to accomplish?

4. There is always more than one method to get what you are after. What is the best method the local can use to try to get what it is after? (*How* should it try to get _____ ?)

   a. What do your top local union officers think is the best method?

   b. Is political action an effective method of achieving the goals of the local? Of unions in general? *Is it a proper method?

5. We have said the local is trying to achieve certain things. Do you feel there are any problems or obstacles which stand in

the way of the local making these achievements? If yes, what are the problems?

  *a. You have mentioned _____ . What causes this problem?

  *b. (INTERVIEWER: if no internal problems have been mentioned, then ask: Are there any problems within the local, the officers, or membership which cause difficulty? If yes, what are the problems?)

6. What problems do you think the top local officers feel are important for the local?

7. Do you know of anything the top local officers have done to try to solve any of the problems facing this local? If yes, what have they done?

  a. Of the things they have done, have any been successful? If yes, what was successful and how was it successful?

  b. What (other) ways do you believe the officers should use to deal with problems?

8. What one thing do you think your top local officers have to worry about most when they have to make an important decision? (Examples: opinions of members; relations with management; economic conditions, etc.)

9. Would you describe any specific happening of which you are aware in which a local union officer did an outstandingly good job or an outstandingly bad job?

10. What do you expect of the top elected officers of your local union?

  a. Do you think the top officers have any problems in trying to live up to what is expected of them? If yes, what problems?

---

  *Asterisks indicate follow-up questions to be asked if relevant.

b. How many hours per week would you guess your top officers spend on union business?

c. What specific types of union business would you guess take the greatest amount of your top officers' time?

*d. What do you think is the most important responsibility of your top local union officers?

e. How well do the officers live up to what is expected of them? (Excellently? Very well? Neither well nor poorly? Rather poorly? Not at all?)

f. What satisfaction do you think your top officers get from holding office?

g. What kind of people are your officers? (How would you describe them?)

11. What in general do officers expect of local union members? What ought they to expect?

a. How well do members live up to what officers expect of them? (Excellently? Very well? Neither well nor poorly? Rather poorly? Not at all?)

b. What satisfactions do members get out of belonging to the union?

*c. Should members participate in the affairs of their local? If yes, what does participation mean to you?

12. What are your rights as a union member? How are your rights protected in this local?

*13. What general responsibilities do local union officers have to the members? Are these responsibilities ever affected or changed by conditions which arise? What conditions?

14. Do you think any group of members in your local is being left out? If yes, what group and why?

15. What in general is expected of the international in your local?

    a. How well does the international live up to what is expected? (Excellently? Very well? Neither well nor poorly? Rather poorly? Not at all?)

    b. How much should the international have to say about how things are run in the local?

16. Does the local have any responsibility to the international? If yes, what is the responsibility?

17. Does the local have any responsibility to management? If yes, what is the responsibility?

18. Does the local have any responsibility to the community? If yes, what is the responsibility?

19. Do unions in general have any responsibility to the federal government? If yes, what is the responsibility?

20. Do unions in general have any responsibility to the general public? If yes, what is the responsibility?

D. Information Questions: Union Members

1. Please indicate your sex. _____ _____
   male   female

2. How old are you?

   | _____ | _____ | _____ | _____ | _____ |
   | under 20 | 20–29 | 30–39 | 40–49 | 50–59 |

   _____
   60 or over

3. What is your marital status?

   | _____ | _____ | _____ |
   | single | married | divorced, widowed, separated |

4. Are you the chief source of income for your household?

   _____ _____
   yes   no

5. How many dependents do you have other than yourself?

   | _____ | _____ | _____ |
   | 2 or less | 3–5 | 6 or more |

6. How many years have you been a member of your local?

   | _____ | _____ | _____ | _____ | _____ | _____ |
   | less than 1 | 1–2 | 3–4 | 5–9 | 10–19 | 20 or more |

7. What is the total number of years you have been a union member?

   _____   _____   _____   _____   _____   _____
   less than 1   1–2   3–4   5–9   10–19   20 or more

8. Are you now a steward or other officer in your local?

   _____   _____
   yes   no

   If your answer is yes, what position do you hold?

   _____

9. Have you been an officer in your local in the past?

   _____   _____
   yes   no

   If you have been an officer, list the positions you have held.

   _____

10. Are you now on any union committees? _____   _____
                                          yes   no

    If you are on any committees, list them.

    _____

11. Have you been on any union committees in the past?

    _____   _____
    yes   no

    If you have been on any committees, list them.

    _____

12. About how many regularly scheduled union meetings have you attended in the last twelve months? _____

13. About how many special meetings of your local have you attended during the last twelve months? _____

14. Did you vote in the last union election for officers?

    _____   _____
     yes   no

15. If you could change one condition which exists within your local, which condition would you change if you wanted to benefit the local most?

    _____

16. Which one of the following outside conditions would you change if you wanted to benefit the local union the most. (Check one.)

    ___ public opinion

    ___ government and laws

    ___ management practices

    ___ economic conditions

    ___ other (Write in.)

    _____

17. Is there any one thing which your local is doing now which it needs to do a better job on in order to become stronger and more effective?

    _____   _____
     yes   no

    If so, what is it? _____

18. How strong is your local in terms of getting what it goes after and accomplishing its aims?

_____	_____	_____	_____	_____
very strong	strong	neither strong nor weak	weak	very weak

19. How much do you think the local president has to say about how things are decided in your local?

_____	_____	_____	_____	_____
a great deal	a fair amount	some	very little	no say at all

20. How much do you think the membership has to say about how things are decided in your local?

_____	_____	_____	_____	_____
a great deal	a fair amount	some	very little	no say at all

21. How much do you think the executive board has to say about how things are decided in your local?

_____	_____	_____	_____	_____
a great deal	a fair amount	some	very little	no say at all

22. How much do you think the bargaining committee has to say about how things are run in your local?

_____	_____	_____	_____	_____
a great deal	a fair amount	some	very little	no say at all

23. Are you employed at the present time? _____   _____
                                          yes   no

24. What is the title of your job in the plant?

_____

Describe briefly what you do in this job.

_____

25. Have you ever been in other occupations? _____   _____

                                                              yes   no

What other *chief* occupations have you had?

_____

26. If you are married, does your wife (husband) work?

    _____   _____

      yes   no

If your wife (husband) does work, what is her (his) occupation?

_____

Is your wife (husband) a union member? _____   _____

                                                          yes   no

Does your wife (husband) approve of union activities?

    _____   _____

      yes   no

27. Was your father a union member? _____   _____

                                                    yes   no

What was your father's usual occupation?

_____

28. Have you ever been unemployed? _____   _____

                                                    yes   no

Have you ever been unemployed for more than thirty days?

    _____   _____

      yes   no

How many times have you been unemployed for more than thirty days?

_____

29. Please check the block below which indicates the amount of schooling you have had.

__ __ __ __ __ __ __ __ Grade School
1   2   3   4   5   6   7   8

__ __ __ __ High School
9 10 11 12

__ __ __ __ College
13 14 15 16

30. What would you say is your chief source of news about union affairs?

_____

31. What would you say is your chief source of news about current events? (Check one.)

__ television

__ radio

__ local newspaper

__ union newspaper

__ magazines

__ other (Write in.)

_____

32. Do you read the union paper regularly? _____   _____
                                              yes   no

What other papers do you read regularly?

_____   _____   _____

none   local newspaper   out-of-town newspaper

33. Do you belong to other organizations besides your union?

_____   _____

yes   no

If you do belong to other organizations, how many of them are there?

_____

34. How well off financially do you think working people are at the present time in the United States?

___ very well off

___ well off

___ medium well off

___ poorly off

___ very poorly off

35. How well off financially do you think working people will be during the next year?

___ very well off

___ well off

___ medium well off

___ poorly off

___ very poorly off

36. How do you expect times will be for your company during. the next year?

— excellent

— good

— medium

— poor

— extremely bad

37. How well off financially do you think working people will be in this community during the next year?

— very well off

— well off

— medium well off

— poorly off

— very poorly off

38. How well off financially do you think you will be during the next year?

— very well off

— well off

— medium well off

— poorly off

— very poorly off

39. Can the government do anything to prevent unemployment resulting from slack business conditions?

   _____   _____
   yes   no

   Can the government prevent unemployment resulting from automation?

   _____   _____
   yes   no

40. Can union members do anything to prevent unemployment resulting from slack business conditions?

   _____   _____
   yes   no

   Can union members prevent unemployment resulting from automation?

   _____   _____
   yes   no

41. *Should* anything be done to prevent unemployment resulting from slack business conditions?

   _____   _____
   yes   no

   Should anything be done to prevent unemployment resulting from automation?

   _____   _____
   yes   no

42. How do you feel about your company as a place to work?

   ___ excellent—always treats workers extremely well

___ good—usually treats workers fairly and squarely

___ fair—neither good nor bad in treatment of workers

___ poor—makes things hard for workers

___ very bad—an extreme enemy of workers

E. Information Questions: Union Officers

1. Please indicate your sex. _____ _____

                                         male   female

2. How old are you?

   _____ _____ _____ _____ _____

   under 20   20–29   30–39   40–49   50–59

   _____

   60 or over

3. What is your marital status?

   _____ _____ _____

   single   married   divorced, widowed, separated

4. Are you the chief source of income for your household?

   _____ _____

   yes   no

5. How many dependents do you have other than yourself?

   _____ _____ _____

   2 or less   3–5   6 or more

6. What is the title of your union office?

   _____

How many years have you held this office?

| less than 1 | 1–2 | 3–4 | 5–9 | 10 or more |

7. How many years have you been a member of your local?

| less than 1 | 1–2 | 3–4 | 5–9 | 10–19 |

20 or more

8. What is the total number of years you have been a union member?

| less than 1 | 1–2 | 3–4 | 5–9 | 10–19 |

20 or more

9. Have you ever held any other office in a union?

| yes | no |

If you have held other union offices, check below any office you have held.

— president

— vice-president

— recording secretary

— financial secretary

— treasurer

— steward or committeeman

___ executive board member

___ other (Write in.)

_____

10. On the average, how many hours per week do you spend on all your union duties combined?

_____	_____	_____	_____	_____	_____
0–9	10–19	20–29	30–39	40–49	50 or more

11. In the past three months, what has been the largest number of hours you have spent on union business in any one week?

_____	_____	_____	_____	_____	_____
0–9	10–19	20–29	30–39	40–49	50 or more

12. In the past three months, what has been the smallest number of hours you have spent on union business in any one week?

_____	_____	_____	_____	_____	_____
0–9	10–19	20–29	30–39	40–49	50 or more

13. If you could change one condition which exists within your local, which condition would you change if you wanted to benefit the local most?

_____

14. Which one of the following outside conditions would you change if you wanted to benefit the local the most? (Check one.)

___ public opinion

___ government and laws

___ management practices

___ economic conditions

___ other (Write in.)

_____

15. Is there any one thing which your local is doing now which
it needs to do a better job on in order to become stronger
and more effective?

_____   _____

yes   no

If so, what is it?

_____

16. How strong is your local in terms of getting what it goes
after and accomplishing its aims?

___ very strong

___ strong

___ neither strong nor weak

___ weak

___very weak

17. How much do you think the local president has to say about
how things are decided in your local?

___ a great deal

___ a fair amount

___ some

___ very little

___ no say at all

18. How much do you think the membership has to say about how things are decided in your local?

___ a great deal

___ a fair amount

___ some

___ very little

___ no say at all

19. How much do you think the executive board has to say about how things are decided in your local?

___ a great deal

___ a fair amount

___ some

___ very little

___ no say at all

20. How much do you think the bargaining committee has to say about how things are run in your local?

___ a great deal

___ a fair amount

___ some

___ very little

___ no say at all

21. What is the title of your job in the plant?

_____

Describe briefly what you do in this job.

_____

22. Have you ever been in other occupations? _____ _____

                                                       yes   no

What other _chief_ occupation have you had?

_____

23. If you are married, does your wife (husband) work?

_____ _____

   yes   no

If your wife (husband) does work, what is her (his) occupation?

_____

Is your wife (husband) a union member? _____ _____

                                      yes   no

Does your wife (husband) approve of your union activity?

_____ _____

   yes   no

24. Was your father a union member? _____ _____

                                yes   no

What was your father's usual occupation?

_____

25. Have you ever been unemployed? _____ _____
                                                 yes   no

    Have you ever been unemployed for more than thirty days?

    _____ _____
     yes   no

    How many times have you been unemployed for more than thirty days? _____

26. Please check the block below which indicates the amount of schooling you have had.

    __ __ __ __ __ __ __ __ Grade School
     1 2 3 4 5 6 7 8

    __ __ __ __ High School
     9 10 11 12

    __ __ __ __ College
     13 14 15 16

27. What would you say is your chief source of news about union affairs?

    _____

28. What would you say is your chief source of news about current events? (Check one.)

    __ television

    __ radio

    __ local newspaper

    __ union newspaper

    __ magazines

— other (Write in.)

_____

29. Do you read the union paper regularly? _____ _____

yes   no

What other papers do you read regularly?

_____ _____ _____

none   local newspaper   out-of-town newspaper

30. What magazines do you read regularly?

— none

— *Reader's Digest* or *Newsweek*

— *Time, U.S. News and World Report,* or *Coronet*

— *Life* or *Look*

— *Saturday Evening Post*

— union magazine

— others (Write in.)

_____

31. Have you read any books within the past six months?

_____ _____

yes   no

If so, how many? _____

32. Do you belong to other organizations besides your union?

_____ _____

yes   no

If you belong to other organizations, to how many do you belong?

_____

Have you ever been an officer in any of these other organizations?

_____   _____

yes   no

If you have been an officer, how many offices have you held?

_____

33. How well off financially do you think working people in the United States are at the present time?

____ very well off

____ well off

____ medium well off

____ poorly off

____ very poorly off

34. How well off financially do you think working people will be during the next year?

____ very well off

____ well off

____ medium well off

____ poorly off

____ very poorly off

35. How do you expect times will be for your company during the next year?

___ excellent

___ good

___ medium

___ poor

___ extremely bad

36. How well off financially do you think working people will be in this community during the next year?

___ very well off

___ well off

___ medium well off

___ poorly off

___ very poorly off

37. How well off financially do you think you will be during the next year?

___ very well off

___ well off

___ medium well off

___ poorly off

___ very poorly off

38. Can the government do anything to prevent unemployment resulting from slack business conditions?

_____   _____
   yes   no

Can the government prevent unemployment resulting from automation?

_____   _____
   yes   no

39. Can union members do anything to prevent unemployment resulting from slack business conditions?

_____   _____
   yes   no

Can union members prevent unemployment resulting from automation?

_____   _____
   yes   no

40. *Should* anything be done to prevent unemployment resulting from slack business conditions?

_____   _____
   yes   no

Should anything be done to prevent unemployment resulting from automation?

_____   _____
   yes   no

41. How do you feel about your company as a place to work?

___ excellent—always treats workers extremely well

— good—usually treats workers fairly and squarely

— fair—neither good nor bad in treatment of workers

— poor—makes things hard for workers

— very bad—an extreme enemy of workers

F. Interview Questions: Union Officers

42. What are the most important responsibilities of your office?
    (As a _____, what are you supposed to worry about, or
    be concerned about?)

    a. What kinds of specific things do you do to try to carry out
       your responsibilities?

       (NOTE: Interviewer to keep at this until at least three
       things are mentioned.)

    *b. Of the things you do, which one thing is the most
        important?

    *c. Why would you rate this as the most important?

43. Of all the things you do as a union officer, which things take
    the most of your time?

       (NOTE: Interviewer to keep at this until at least three
       things are mentioned.)

    *a. Would you estimate what per cent of your union time is
        taken by each of these things?

       (NOTE: Interviewer to summarize things mentioned.)

b. On your questionnaire you indicated you spent _____
hours on union business in a recent heavy week and
_____ hours in a recent slack week. What explains the
difference between these weeks?

c. Would it be possible to spend fewer hours on union
business than you normally spend? If no, why not? If yes,
in what way?

44. What are the goals, or aims, of your local? (What is your
local after? What is it trying to do?) Were the aims of
your local ever different in the past? If yes, what were the
differences and why did they exist?

45. What aims do you think your members want the local to
accomplish? How do you find out what they want?

46. What aims do you think the international wants the local to
accomplish? How do you find out what the international
wants?

47. Now, you have mentioned some goals for your local. There
has to be a method of achieving those goals. What is the
best method the local can use to try to achieve its goals?

a. What do members think are the best methods of achieving
the union's goals?

b. Is political action an effective method of achieving the
goals of the local? Of unions in general?

*c. Do your members tend to approve of political action?

48. You have mentioned some goals the local is trying to achieve.
What problems do you feel are the greatest hindrances, or
barriers, to the achievement of these goals?

*a. You have mentioned _____. What causes this problem?

(NOTE: Interviewer to summarize problems mentioned.)

*b. Were your problems ever different in the past? If yes, what were the differences and why did they exist?

*c. (NOTE TO INTERVIEWER: If no internal problems have been mentioned, then ask, Are there any problems within the local or within the membership which cause difficulty? If yes, what are the problems?)

49. Do the members feel that the local has any problems? If yes, what problems do they see?

50. What problems does the international think this local has? How do you find out what problems the international sees?

51. How have you tried to solve or lessen the problems you have in the local?

   (NOTE: Interviewer may have to summarize actions already mentioned.)

   a. Of the actions you have taken, which have been most successful in actually solving the problems? In what way were actions successful?

   b. Can you think of any different ways in which you might have dealt with your problems? If yes, what are they and why were they not used?

52. How do newly elected union officers learn to recognize their important problems and how to deal with them?

   (NOTE: Interviewer may have to ask, How did you learn to recognize and deal with problems?)

53. What one thing do you have to worry about above all others when an important decision has to be made? (examples: opinions of members or other persons; relations with management; economic conditions)

54. Would you describe any specific instance of which you are aware in which a local union officer performed in an especially effective way or in an especially ineffective way?

55. What, in general, is expected of the top elected officers by the members? By the international?

    a. How well do the officers live up to what is expected of them? Excellently? Very well? Neither well nor poorly? Rather poorly? Not at all?)

    b. What satisfactions do officers gain from being officers?

    c. Do the members feel the officers have any problems? If yes, what problems?

56. What, in general, is expected of the members of your local?

    a. How well do members live up to what is expected of them? (Excellently? Very well? Neither well nor poorly? Rather poorly? Not at all?)

    *b. Most union officials expect their members to participate. Would you give us a complete picture of what you think participation really means?

    c. What kind of people are your members? (How would you describe your members?)

57. Your members, of course, have certain rights under your constitution. How well do the members understand their rights? How are the rights of the members protected in your local?

58. What general responsibility do local union officers have to the members? Are these responsibilities ever affected or changed by conditions which arise? What conditions?

59. Do you think any group of members in your local is being left out? If yes, what group and why?

60. What, in general, is expected of the international in your local?

    a. How well does the international live up to what is expected? (Excellently? Very well? Neither well nor poorly? Rather poorly? Not at all?)

    b. How much should the international have to say about how things are run in the local?

61. Does the local have any responsibility to the international? If yes, what is the responsibility?

62. Does the local have any responsibility to management? If yes, what is the responsibility?

63. Does the local have any responsibility to the community? If yes, what is the responsibility?

64. Do unions in general have any responsibility to the federal government? If yes, what is the responsibility?

65. Do unions in general have any responsibility to the general public? If yes, what is the responsibility?

Bibliography

Bibliographie

Bibliography

ALEXANDER, J. W., and BERGER, M. "Grass-Roots Labor Leader," in *Studies in Leadership*, ed. A. W. GOULDNER. New York: Harper and Bros., 1950.

ALINSKY, SAUL. *John L. Lewis: An Unauthorized Biography*. New York: G. P. Putnam Sons, 1949.

ARGYRIS, C. *Personality and Organization*. New York: Harper and Bros., 1957.

ALLPORT, G. W. "The Psychology of Participation," *Psychological Review*, LIII (1945), 117–32.

BAKKE, E. W. "Why Workers Join Unions," *Personnel*, XXII (1945), 37–46.

BAKKE, E. W.; KERR, CLARK; and ANROD, CHARLES W. *Unions, Management and the Public*. New York: Harcourt, Brace, and Co., 1960.

BARBASH, JACK. *The Practice of Unionism*. New York: Harper and Bros., 1956.

–––––. *Unions and Union Leadership*. New York: Harper and Bros., 1959.

–––––. *Universities and Unions in Workers' Education*. New York: Harper and Bros., 1955.

BARBER, B. "Participation and Mass Apathy in Associations," in *Studies in Leadership*, ed. A. W. GOULDNER. New York: Harper and Bros., 1950.

BARKIN, SOLOMON. *The Decline of the Labor Movement*. New York: Fund for the Republic, 1962.

Bass, Bernard M. *Leadership, Psychology and Organizational Behavior.* New York: Harper and Bros., 1960.

Brooks, George. *Sources of Vitality in the American Labor Movement.* (New York State School of Industrial and Labor Relations Bulletin No. 41.) Ithaca, N.Y., 1960.

Centers, R. "Attitude and Belief in Relation to Occupational Stratification," *Journal of Social Psychology,* XXVII (1948), 159–85.

————. "Motivational Aspects of Occupational Stratification," *Journal of Social Psychology,* XXVIII (1948), 187–217.

Chalfen, L. "The Psychological Effects of Unionism on the Member," *Journal of Social Psychology,* XXV (1947), 133–37.

Chinoy, Ely. "Local Union Leadership," in *Studies in Leadership,* ed. A. W. Gouldner. New York: Harper and Bros., 1950.

————. "The Tradition of Opportunity and the Aspirations of Automobile Workers," *American Journal of Sociology,* LVII (1952), 453–59.

Coleman, John R. "The Compulsive Pressures of Democracy in Unionism," *American Journal of Sociology,* LXI, May, 1956.

Commons, John R. *The Economics of Collective Action.* New York: Macmillan Co., 1951.

Dean, Lois R. "Social Integration, Attitudes, and Union Activity," *Industrial and Labor Relations Review,* VIII (1954–55), 48–58.

————. "Union Activity and Dual Loyalty," *Industrial and Labor Relations Review,* VII (1953–54), 526–36.

Dunnette, M. D., and Uphoff, W. H. "Union Attitudes and Membership Participation," *Business News Notes* (School of Business Administration, University of Minnesota), June 1, 1955, pp. 1–3.

Fromm, Erich. *The Sane Society.* New York: Rinehart, 1955.

Gibb, Cecil A. "Leadership," in *Handbook of Social Psychology,* Vol. II, ed. Gardner Lindzey. Reading, Mass.: Addison, Wesley Publishing Co., 1954.

Ginzberg, Eli. *The Labor Leader: An Exploratory Study.* New York: Macmillan Co., 1948.

Golden, Clinton S., and Ruttenberg, Harold J. *The Dynamics of Industrial Democracy.* New York: Harper and Bros., 1942.

Gouldner, A. W. "Attitudes of 'Progressive' Trade Union Leaders," *American Journal of Sociology,* LII (1947), 389–92.

———— (ed.). *Studies in Leadership.* New York: Harper and Bros., 1950.

HARDMAN, J. B. S., and NEUFELD, MAURICE F. *The House of Labor.* New York: Prentice-Hall, 1951.

HEARD, ALEXANDER. *The Costs of Democracy.* Garden City, N.Y.: Anchor Books, 1962.

HEMPHILL, JOHN K. *Theory of Leadership.* Columbus, O.: Ohio State University Personnel Research Board, 1952.

HERZBERG, FREDERICK; MAUSNER, BERNARD; and SNYDERMAN, BARBARA. *The Motivation to Work.* New York: John Wiley and Sons, 1959.

HOMANS, GEORGE. *The Human Group.* New York: Harcourt, Brace, and Co., 1950.

HOWE, IRVING, and WIDICK, B. J. *The UAW and Walter Reuther.* New York: Random House, 1949.

HOXIE, R. F. *Trade Unionism in the United States.* New York: D. Appleton and Co., 1917.

IMBERMAN, A. A. "Labor Leaders and Society," *Harvard Business Review,* XXVIII (1950), 52–60.

JACOBS, PAUL. *The State of the Union.* New York: Atheneum Publishers, 1963.

JOSEPHSON, MATTHEW. *Sidney Hillman: Statesman of American Labor.* New York: Doubleday and Co., 1952.

KARSH, B., and LONDON, J. "The Coal Miners: A Study of Union Control," *Quarterly Journal of Economics,* LXVIII (1954), 415–36.

KATZ, DANIEL. "Satisfactions and Deprivations in Industrial Life," in *Industrial Conflict,* eds. A. KORNHAUSER; R. DUBIN; and A. M. Ross. New York: McGraw-Hill Book Co., 1954.

KORNHAUSER, A. "Human Motivations Underlying Industrial Conflict," in *Industrial Conflict,* eds. A. KORNHAUSER; R. DUBIN; and A. M. Ross. New York: McGraw-Hill Book Co., 1954.

KORNHAUSER, A.; SHEPPARD, H. L.; and MAYER, A. J. *When Labor Votes.* New York: University Books, 1956.

KOVNER, J., and LAHNE, H. J. "Shop Society and the Union," *Industrial and Labor Relations Review,* VII (1953–54), 3–14.

KRECH, DAVID; CRUTCHFIELD, RICHARD S.; and BALLACHEY, EDGER-
TON, L. *Individual in Society*. New York: McGraw-Hill Book
Co., 1962.

KYLLONEN, T. W. "Social Characteristics of Active Unionists,"
American Journal of Sociology, LVI (1950–51), 528–33.

LEISERSON, WILLIAM M. *American Trade Union Democracy*. New
York: Columbia University Press, 1951.

LENS, SIDNEY. *The Crisis of American Labor*. New York: Sagamore
Press, 1959.

LESTER, RICHARD A. *As Unions Mature*. Princeton, N. J.: Princeton
University Press, 1958.

LIPSET, SEYMOUR MARTIN, and GORDON, J. "Mobility and Trade
Union Membership," in *Class, Status, and Power*, eds. R. BENDIX
and S. M. LIPSET. Glencoe, Ill.: Free Press of Glencoe, 1953.

LIPSET, SEYMOUR MARTIN; TROW, MARTIN A.; and COLEMAN,
JAMES S. *Union Democracy*. Garden City, N.Y.: Anchor Books,
1962.

MACDONALD, LOIS. *Leadership Dynamics and the Trade-Union
Leader*. New York: New York University Press, 1959.

MASLOW, ABRAHAM. *Motivation and Personality*. New York: Harper
and Bros., 1954.

McGREGOR, DOUGLAS. *The Human Side of Enterprise*. New York:
McGraw-Hill Book Co., 1960.

MICHELS, ROBERT. *Political Parties*. Translated by EDEN PAUL and
CEDAR PAUL, with an Introduction by SEYMOUR MARTIN LIPSET.
New York: Collier Books, 1962.

MILLER, GLENN W., and ROSEN, NED. "Members' Attitudes toward
the Shop Steward," *Industrial and Labor Relations Review*, X
(1957), 516–31.

MILLER, GLENN W., and STOCKTON, EDWARD J. "Local Union
Officer—His Background, Activities and Attitudes," *Labor Law
Journal*, VIII (1957), 28–29.

MILLS, C. WRIGHT. *The New Men of Power*. New York: Harcourt,
Brace, and Co., 1948.

————. *The Power Elite*. New York: Oxford University Press,
1959.

PERLMAN, SELIG. *A Theory of the Labor Movement.* New York: Macmillan Co., 1929.

PETERSON, FLORENCE. "Cause of Industrial Unrest," *Annals of the American Academy of Political and Social Science,* CCLXXIV (March, 1951), 25–31.

PHELPS, O. W. "Community Recognition of Union Leaders," *Industrial and Labor Relations Review,* VII (1953–54), 419–33.

POLANYI, KARL. *The Great Transformation.* Boston: Beacon Press, 1957.

PURCELL, T. V. *Blue Collar Man.* Cambridge, Mass.: Harvard University Press, 1960.

————. "Dual Allegiance to Company and Union—Packing House Workers," *Personnel Psychology,* VII (1954), 48–58.

————. *The Worker Speaks His Mind on Company and Union.* Cambridge, Mass.: Harvard University Press, 1953.

REMMERS, L. J., and REMMERS, H. H. "Studies in Industrial Empathy, (I): Labor Leaders' Attitudes toward Industrial Supervision and Their Estimate of Managements' Attitudes," *Personnel Psychology,* II (1949), 427–36.

RIECKEN, HENRY W., and HOMANS, GEORGE C. "Psychological Aspects of Social Structure," in *Handbook of Social Psychology,* Vol. II, ed. GARDNER LINDZEY. Reading, Mass.: Addison, Wesley Publishing Co., 1954.

ROSE, ARNOLD M. *Union Solidarity.* Minneapolis: University of Minnesota Press, 1952.

ROSEN, HJALMAR, and ROSEN, R. A. *The Union Member Speaks.* New York: Prentice-Hall, 1955.

SAYLES, LEONARD R., and STRAUSS, GEORGE. *The Local Union: Its Place in the Industrial Plant.* New York: Harper and Bros., 1953.

SEIDMAN, J. "Democracy in Labor Unions," *Journal of Political Economy,* LXI (1943), 221–31.

SEIDMAN, J.; LONDON, JACK; and KARSH, BERNARD. "Leadership in a Local Union," *American Journal of Sociology,* LVI (1950–51), 229–37.

――――. "Political Consciousness in a Local Union," *Public Opinion Quarterly*, XV (1951), 692–702.

――――. "Why Workers Join Unions," *Annals of the American Academy of Political and Social Science*, CCLXXIV (March, 1951), 75–84.

SEIDMAN, J.; LONDON, JACK; KARSH, BERNARD; and TAGLIACOZZO, DAISY L. *The Worker Views His Union*. Chicago: University of Chicago Press, 1958.

SHARTLE, CARROLL L. *Executive Performances and Leadership*. Englewood Cliffs, N.J.: Prentice-Hall, 1956.

SHEPARD, H. A. "Democratic Control in a Labor Union," *American Journal of Sociology*, LIV (1949), 311–16.

SHERIF, M., and CANTRIL, H. *The Psychology of Ego Involvements*. New York: John Wiley and Sons, 1947.

SPROTT, W. J. H. *Human Groups*. Baltimore: Penguin Books, 1958.

STOGDILL, RALPH M. *Individual Behavior and Group Achievement*. London: Oxford University Press, 1959.

STRAUSS, GEORGE. "The Shifting Power Balance in the Plant," *Industrial Relations*, I, No. 3 (May, 1962), 79.

STRAUSS, GEORGE, and SAYLES, L. R. "The Local Union Meeting," *Industrial and Labor Relations Review*, VI (1952–53), 206–19.

――――. "Patterns of Participation in Local Unions," *Industrial and Labor Relations Review*, VI (1952–53), 31–43.

TAFT, PHILIP. "Ideologies and Industrial Conflict," in *Industrial Conflict*, eds. A. KORNHAUSER; R. DUBIN; and A. M. Ross. New York: McGraw-Hill Book Co., 1954.

――――. *The Structure and Government of Trade Unions*. Cambridge, Mass.: Harvard University Press, 1954.

TANNENBAUM, ARNOLD S., and KAHN, ROBERT L. *Participation in Union Locals*. Evanston, Ill.: Row, Peterson, and Co., 1953.

WEISSKOPF, W. A. "Industrial Institutions and Personality Structure," *Journal of Social Issues*, VII, No. 4 (1951), 1–6.

WOLFENSTEIN, MARTHA. "The Emergence of Fun Morality," *Journal of Social Issues*, VII, No. 4 (1951), 15–25.

Index

Administration: differences in unions, 157; time consumed in, 13, 82, 111

Age range of officers, 76

Agricultural background of members, 33–34

Allegiance of members, 105, 116; dual allegiance, 126

American Federation of Labor, 167

Attendance at meetings, 138, 190; by officers, 80, 82, 83; rewards for, 108, 114, 118; stimulation of, 106–7

Attitudes: of employers, 34–37; of members of unions, 33–34, 124, 181; of public, toward unions, 24

Automation, effects of, 125, 136, 193

Backgrounds of members, influence of, 33–34

Bargaining: centralization of, 151, 194; control of, 28; factors in success of, 100–101, 105; members' view of, 127; unimportance of, 146

Behavioral definition of leadership, 15–17

Benefits, improvement of, 90, 92

Centralization of union functions, 151, 194

Changing conditions, officers' awareness of, 135–37

Changing role of officers, 187

Changing wants of members, 93, 166, 185, 193

Class interests, 172

Coal miners, attitudes of, 33–34, 155

Cohesion, organizational, 31, 61, 180

Colleges, training programs in, 197–201

Communications in unions, 64–69, 141–43; about international unions, 29, 68, 92; about union affairs, 66; between members and officers, 67, 175, 193; differences in, 158–60; distortion in, 68; inefficiency in, 67; need for improvement of, 190–91; sources of information in, 158

Community affecting leadership policies, 23–25

Concepts of unionism: by members, 43–60, 123–29, 159; by officers, 89–97, 134–40

Conflicts: among union members, 133; between company and union, 128

Congress of Industrial Organizations, 167

Conservative outlook of union members, 168

Contract negotiations: and attitude of employers, 145; centralization of, 151, 194; time spent on, 84, 87–88; *see also* Bargaining

Control: of members, levels of, 157–58; over officers, 175

Creativity, need for, 188

Crisis situations, results of, 179–80

Customs and habits; *see* Traditional attitudes

Decline of unions, 171

Definition: of group, 18; of leadership, 14, 17, 119; of organization, 18

Democracy in unions, 39–40, 121–23, 172–78

Differences among local unions, 69–73, 92, 96, 102, 111; contrasting patterns in two unions, 152–62

Displacement from jobs, fear of, 47, 147

Dynamics of local unionism, 4

Economic conditions: affecting unions, 170; effects of, 135, 147; of employers, 36–37, 147

Education: of members, 32, 47–48; of officers, 76, 139, 140, 194, 195–204; training for leadership, 30, 140, 156, 195–204; vocational, 198, 199, 200

Educational programs for members, 107, 109–10, 192; offered by international union, 29–30, 197

Elected officials, behavior of, 16–17

Election of officers, 121–23, 173–74

Employers: adverse influence of, 112; attitudes of, 34–37; concessions of, 48; difficulties with, 155–56; economic position of, 36–37, 147; influencing leadership performance of officers, 144–48; interaction with union members, 50; members' attitude toward, 34, 124; obligations of, 127; officers' approach to, 107, 111; opinions of, affecting officers, 123; union-management relationship, 100–101, 105, 126, 127

Environmental factors affecting leadership policies, 23–38; the community, 23–25; employers, 34–37; international unions, 25–30; local unions, 30–34

Experience, as method of learning by officers, 139

Factionalism in unions, 71, 102, 133, 155

Farmers, attitudes of, 33–34

Geographic location, effects of, 23–25

Geographic origins of members, differences in, 33–34

Goals of members, 19, 42, 44–49; attempts to remove barriers to, 106–13, 156; changes in, 93, 166, 185, 193; identification of problems by officers, 97–106; importance of positive goals, 161–62; means for accomplishing, 53; as perceived by officers, 89–97; problems preventing achievement of, 19–20

Grievance-settlement process, 36; attitude of members toward, 114–15; as group goal, 114–15, 117; time required for, 80–83, 111, 128, 145

Group: definition of, 18; external rewards of membership in, 116, 192; internal rewards of membership in, 116, 190; relationship of members in, 42; satisfactions derived from, 60–64, 106, 114, 117, 118, 184, 189

Growth of unions, prerequisites for, 179–82

Humanities, training in, 198–201

Indoctrination of members, 110

Industrial backgrounds of members, 33

Information, dissemination of; *see* Communication

Information questions: for members, 241–50; for officers, 251–62

Institutional approach to unionism, 5–6

Interaction between officers and members, 39–40, 163, 175

International unions, 25–30; in bargaining process, 28; centralization of functions in, 151–52, 194; communication with members, 159; education programs of, 29–30, 197; members' concept of, 53, 57–58; publications of, 29, 92; relationships with local union, 148–50; service and supervision from, 26–28, 150, 156; sources of information about, 68; view of local union problems, 104–5

Interviews: with members, 213–14, 237–40; with officers, 211–12, 263–67

Labor relations, trends in, 150–52

Leadership: behavioral definition of, 15–17; components of, 18–20; contrasting patterns in two unions, 152–62; definition of, 14–15, 17, 119; elected officials, 16–17; environmental factors affecting policies, 23–38; interactional theory of, 39–40, 163, 175; need for followers, 41–42; process of, 4–5; qualities lacking in officers, 113, 118, 195; social leaders, 13; training for, 30, 140, 156, 195–204; unsuccessful, causes for, 121–64; *see also* Officers

Legal standing of union organizations, 169

Legalism: of employers, 36, 145; in unions, 72

Legislation: prolabor and social welfare, 167; regulating unions, 169; state-enacted, 24–25; unfavorable, effects of, 101–2

Liberalism, political, 168

Limitations of officers, 134–44

Local unions: differences among, 69–73, 92, 96, 102, 111; qualities of, 30–34; relationships with international union, 148–50

Maintenance function of leaders, 119

Management; *see* Employers

Members: allegiance of, 105, 116, 126; attitudes toward employers, 124; attitudes toward unions, 181; basic wants of, 189; changing wants of, 93, 166, 185, 193; communication with officers, 142, 175, 193; concepts compared with officers' views, 94–96; concepts of international union, 53, 57–58, 159; concepts of unionism, 43–60, 123–29; conflicts among, 133; control of, 157–58; education levels of, 32, 47–48; educational programs for, 107, 109–10, 192; expectations of, 40, 58–59; fear of management reprisal, 47, 147; geographic origins of, 33–34; goals of, 19, 42, 44–49, 188–89; higher order wants of, 188–89; image of officers' role, 85; inactivity of, 97–100, 104–5, 114–15, 118, 165; indoctrination of, 110; interaction with company, 50; interaction with officers, 39–40; interdependence of, 42; interviews with, 213–14, 237–40; means preferred to accomplish goals, 53; minority guarantees, 173–74; officers' views of, 97–100, 138; opinions of, affecting officers, 123; orientation of, 42, 64, 171; participation in union affairs, 55–57, 103–4, 131–32, 182–94; personal characteristics of, 31–32; personal problems of, 130, 145, 193, 194; power demonstrations of, 56; pressures from, 121–31; problems identified by, 49–52; protection of, 45, 58, 90, 92, 115, 123; questionnaire for, 215–36, 241–50; racial differences of, 32–33; relations with employers, 145–47; relations with officers, 129–31; relationship to union, 6, 10; rewards of group membership, 116, 190, 192; satisfaction from union activities, 60–64, 106, 114, 117, 118, 184, 189; size of membership, 30–31; skills of, 31; social consciousness of, 45; solidarity of, 112, 132–33, 156; traditions and outlooks of, 33–34; unemployment of, 46–47; see also Goals; Participation

Method of study of unions, 211–14

Miners, attitudes of, 33–34, 155

Minority guarantees, 173–74

Movement unionism, 91, 203

News media, influence of, 25

Newspapers of international unions, 29

Objectives of study, 21

Officers: abilities of, 51–52; activities considered most important, 83–84; activities requiring most time, 79–83; administrative activities of, 13, 82, 111; age range of, 76; approach to management problem, 107, 111; attendance at meetings, 80, 82, 83; awareness of change, 135–37; behavior in office, 76–86; busy weeks and slack weeks of, 77–79, 85; as candidates for election, 174; causes of unsuccessful leadership, 121–64; changing role of, 187; characteristics of, 13, 75–76, 160, 166; circumscribed concepts of, 41, 135, 137; communications problems, 64–69, 141–43, 175, 193; concepts compared with members' views, 94–96;

concepts of democracy, 176; concepts of members' role, 138; concepts of responsibilities of office, 83, 86–89; concepts of unionism, 89–97, 134–40; and conflicts between company and union, 128; control exercised by, 12; customs and habits of, 139, 195; demands on, 195; educating members, 107, 109–10; education of, 76, 139, 140, 194, 195–204; employers affecting leadership performance of, 123, 144–48; experience as method of learning, 139; factors considered when making decisions, 123; functions of, 11–12, 86, 137, 145; grievance handling by, 36, 80–83, 111, 114–15, 117, 128, 145; identification of barriers to goal achievement, 97–106, 156; interaction with members, 10, 20, 39–40, 163, 175; interviews with, 211–12, 263–67; as labor relations practitioner, 128; lack of training and skills, 140–43; lacking leadership qualities, 113, 118, 195; as leaders, 75–120; maintenance role of, 119; management opinions affecting, 123; members' expectations for, 58–59, 85; members' opinions affecting, 123; membership in other organizations, 139; motivations of, 13–14, 39; narrow range of problem-solving behavior, 110–11; negotiating contracts, 84, 87–88; orientation of, 13, 88, 92, 93, 171; perceptions of union goals, 89–97; personal limitations of, 134–44; personal services given by, 130, 145, 193, 194; personality and interpersonal relations, 143–44; preoccupation with local aims, 92; pressure on, 12; problems with membership, 97–100; questionnaire for, 251–62; relationship with management, 100–101, 105, 127; relationship with members, 97–100, 129–31; replacement of, by voting, 173; solving problems in goal achievement, 106–13, 156; sources of information about, 67; stimulating member participation, 106–7, 138, 143, 182–94; studies of, 7–10; task function of, 119; time spent on union duties, 77–83; traditional attitudes of, 135, 137, 195; training of, 156; *see also* Leadership

Organization: cohesion in, 31, 61, 180; definition of, 18; relationship of members in, 42; satisfactions derived from, 61, 106, 114, 117, 118, 184, 189

Orientation: of leaders, 13, 88, 92; of members, 42, 64, 171; of officers, 93, 171

Participation of members in union affairs, 55–57, 131–32, 138; lack of, 97–100, 104–5, 114–15, 118, 165; rewards in, 108, 114, 116–17, 118, 190, 192; as source of satisfaction, 60–64, 106, 114, 117, 118, 184, 189; stimulation of, 106–7, 138, 143, 182–94

Pattern bargaining, role of, 151–52

Personal characteristics: of leaders, 13; of members, 31–32; of officers, 143–44, 160, 166

Personal contacts, for communication, 66, 72

Personal services demanded of officers, 130, 145, 193, 194

Philosophy of union members, 203–4

Political action of unions, 167–70

Power demonstrations, effects of, 56

Pressures from members, effects of, 121–31

Problems preventing goal achievement, 19–20, 156; attempts to remove barriers, 106–13; identified by members, 49–52; identified by officers, 97–106; validity of, 103

Productivity of union members, 50

Protection of members, desire for, 45, 58, 90, 92, 115, 123

Psychology of groups, 183

Public attitudes toward unions, 24

Publications: of international unions, 29, 68, 92; relating to unions, 5–10

Questionnaire: for members, 215–36, 241–50; for officers, 251–62

Racial differences in unions, 32–33

Recognition, need for, 188

Responsibilities of officers, 83, 86–89

Rewards for member participation, 108, 114, 116–17, 118, 190, 192

Satisfactions members derive from unionism, 60–64, 106, 114, 117, 118, 184, 189

Security, need for, 186

Self-expression, need for, 188

Size of local unions, 30–31

Skills: lack of, in officers, 140–43; of members, 31

Social consciousness of union members, 45

Social recognition, need for, 188

Social sciences, training in, 198–201

Socioeconomic backgrounds of members, 31–34

Solidarity in unions, 156; importance of, 112; lack of, 132–33

State-enacted legislation, 24–25

Stewards, role of, 192

Strike, wildcat, 147, 155

Structure of unions, 72

Survival of unions, prerequisites for, 179–82

Task function of leaders, 119

Time spent by officers for union duties, 77–83

Traditional attitudes: of members, 33–34; of officers, 135, 137, 139, 166, 195

Training for leadership, 30, 140, 156, 195–204; *see also* Education

Unemployment, affecting attitudes of members, 46–47

Union-movement philosophy, 91, 203

Unionism: criticisms of, 181, 206; decline of, 171; dynamics of, 4; forces against, 171; future role of, 167–79; institutional approach to, 5–6; members' concepts of, 123–29; narrow interests in, 172; officers' concepts of, 134–40; original values in,

180; potential of, 182; prerequisites for survival and growth of, 179–82; public image of, 181

Universities, training programs in, 197–201

Unsuccessful leadership, causes of, 121–64

Vocational education, 198, 199, 200

Voting power of members, effects of, 121–23, 173

Wages: future possible gains in, 117; improvement of, 88, 90, 92, 94–96, 186, 192

Working conditions: future possible gains in, 117; improvement of, 88, 90, 92, 192